KASABIAN
Sound, Movement & Empire

Published in 2008 by
INDEPENDENT MUSIC PRESS
Independent Music Press is an imprint of I.M. P. Publishing Limited
This Work is Copyright © I. M. P. Publishing Ltd 2005

Kasabian: Sound, Movement And Empire
by Joe Shooman

British Library Cataloguing-in-Publication Data.
A catalogue for this book is available from The British Library.

ISBN 978-1-906191-00-9 & 1-906191-00-X

Cover Design by Fresh Lemon.
Edited by Martin Roach.

Printed in the UK.

Independent Music Press
P.O. Box 69, Church Stretton, Shropshire SY6 6WZ

Visit us on the web at: www.impbooks.com

For a free catalogue, e-mail us at: info@impbooks.com
Fax: 01694 720049

KASABIAN
Sound, Movement & Empire

Independent Music Press

Contents

Acknowledgements

A massive thank you to everyone who contributed and shared their insight into this story. I'm extremely grateful for the time and trouble taken by a host of characters who could have quite easily used words of four letters when I approached them for this project. But very few did, so let's get in the zone with the interviewees, totally empire one and all. God bless: Jim Abbiss, Ian Abraham, Simon Barnicott, James Barton, Ryan Bernstein, Joe Betts, Rupert Browne, Jersey Budd, Phil Bunford, Ben Cole, Kim Dawson, Martin Fougerol, Scott Gilbert, Joana Glaza, Mitch Glover, Ryan Glover, Ash Hanning, John Hoare, Mike Jonns, Jagz Kooner, Garret 'Jacknife' Lee, Scott Lyon, Keiron Mahon, Amanda McGowan, Joanna Swan, Arthur Tapp, James Milton Thompson, Pete Oag, Karen Pirie, Nick Raymonde, Neil Ridley, Andy Stone, Joanna Swan, Eddy Temple-Morris, Alex Thomas, Mark Vidler, Trevor Wensley.

For help, advice, contacts, suggestions and/or access to unique and archive material including interviews, reminiscences, photo suggestions and general supporting material, a huge thank you to the clever convicts: Neil Barclay, Michy Brooks, Duncan Bryceland, Matt Cartmell, Ian Clifford, Scott Colothan, James Currie, Andy Day, Rachel Dejnowycz, Shari Denson, Niall Doherty, Jonathan Dumpleton, JJ Dunning, Tank Ernst, Hannah Hamilton, Danielle Hinde, Andy Inglis, Alec James Joyce, Lindsey Kent, Fiona McKinlay, Will Kinsman, 3. M. Kurz, Beatriz Lopez, Rocky Mademann, Davinia Mann, Lucy Matthews, Heike Schneider-Matzigkeit, Fraser Nicolson, Gill Nightingale, Mat Ong, Rumi Oyama, Nick Pittom, Justin Pritchard, Raziq Rauf, Julian Ridgway, Andrew Roberts, Jon Sanders, Paul Scaife, Paul Shefrin, Lisa Southern, Giles Stubbings, Lauren Tones, Massimiliano Trentin, Janine Warren, Michael Whelan, Yuri Yamafuji.

Nuff 'spect to Andy Black of Pineaapster for his consistently helpful suggestions and patience in answering my increasingly complex questions, help with contacts and all manner of great things – you went way beyond the call of duty and I'm very grateful. Nice one mate. Good vibrations to Tom McCarthy, keep 'em in line, mate, and make sure the licences are up to date, we all know who really runs the BBC.

If, as seems inevitable, I've forgotten anyone, please accept my sincerest apologies and assurances that it's only my hungover brain playing tricks on me, and nowt more sinister than that.

Thanks as ever to Mart and Dave at Independent Music Press, and to Jon Hall and Kenn Taylor for the transcriptions. Loads of love to Mam and Dad and a huge hello to all of the brand old and brand new Shoomans. Yn enwedig, croeso cynnes i Owen bach, and to the lovely Suzy Faulkner, merci beaucoup, beaucoup, beaucoup pour tout.

Special thanks to Kim Dawson for her fantastic ideas and support of Independent Music Press.

When I was a young kid at Cae Top I thought Mr. McBryde was a giant but I didn't fully appreciate how true that was 'til I grew up. Diolch yn enfawr am bopeth. Sadly, I never got to buy Tony that curry I promised him, and to David, I know you have found peace where you are, and plenty of chocolate milkshakes to wash it down, too.
Good souls, forever.

Joe Shooman, February 2008

Foreword

It's so wonderful to know that we have another up and coming big name on the horizon from Leicester. I am proud to be from Leicester. I was brought up in Highfields and playing football on the streets was a common sight at that time. We had a garage repair shop opposite our house which had a large door we used as a goal. It was a lot of fun.

I started singing in working men's clubs at the early age of seventeen, and it served me as a great apprenticeship for what was to happen later on in my life. It was a great foundation that stood me in good stead and a wonderful beginning. I have watched *X-Factor* and seen some amazing talent. The opportunity these young people are getting is truly a great one. They have to make sure it's not too fast a beginning. The places I played to get experience are non-existent now, so these young contestants must 'rehearse' at home. But, you must sing in front of an audience to realise whether you are being appreciated or not. Standing in front of a crowd and singing is a whole different ball game.

I'm extremely happy and proud that Kasabian have got to where they are by working hard, and not being discovered quickly by an *X-Factor* or shows of that sort, because experience, performance, charisma and stage presence are all important factors. Kasabian seem to have done the rounds and lots of homework in order to get where they have. They have travelled round the country picking up a fan base which is so important, and that's how it all began for me. I used to hang out in Tin Pan Alley in London looking for work with a few musicians in a broken-down old van that I picked up for £11, and that got us around to pubs, clubs, and a place to sleep at night.

At the age of twenty eight, luck came my way with a song called 'Release Me'. It sold two and a half million in six weeks and went to Number 1 around the world. In fact, my first concert in Leicester with my newborn hit was with the Walker Brothers and Jimi Hendrix. I was special guest star. The next time I worked with Jimi, he opened and I closed. It was a great honour being on the same bill with one of my favourite people.

In today's world, it's quite impossible to achieve international fame immediately like it was then when it happened to me. You had people pushing buttons for you, getting radio play, people from your record company going to radio stations pushing your product like crazy.

Now it's a whole new world. There are not many big record companies left and major talents are neglected because the music industry has reached a saturation point. It's such a computerised world that even the general public no longer knows who is Number 1 in the charts. At one time, when people like Fluffy Freeman, Jimmy Saville and other super DJs were around, they really gave you a good kick start. In today's world, performers really have to get out there and do a lot of interviews – press, radio shows and TV – to get their faces and names out there. I thank a lot of my fans because, to me, they are the spark plugs of my success. They are your cheerleaders who stimulate the audience with their enthusiasm.

I would like to share this advice with Kasabian … take the success you have and study your hit formula. Make sure your future choices of releases are well chosen. Lastly, be careful how you take care of business, because it's easy to lose what you have strived for in a heartbeat … a Leicester Heartbeat. So take care, my friends!

People ask me, 'When are you going to hang your hat up?' and I say 'I love what I am doing and as long as my fans want me, I shall be there for them.' I love to travel and my vocation and luck in the industry has afforded me the luxury of travelling around the world doing what I truly enjoy. When I feel the warmth of an audience, there is no better feeling. I always say applause is the food of an artist, and thank you for not starving me.

Good luck, Kasabian, Leicester and I are proud of YOU.

Sincerely,

Engelbert Humperdinck

SOUND

CHAPTER ONE

Early Doors

Leicester is a rather unassuming town in the middle of the UK. It has some houses, a college, a few venues and all the usual stuff you'd expect of a provincial conurbation. Depending on how you look at it, the population's either a quarter or half of a million, the latter figure taking into account the urban area that surrounds the city proper, places like Glensfield, Wigston and Blaby (somewhere we're going to hear rather a lot about as we go on). Either way, it's the tenth most populated city in England, which as statistics go is rather an unimpressive one. Leicester has a long and noble history, having been founded by one King Leir, an ancient Briton whose story later inspired William Shakespeare to write his play of – more or less – the same name. Leicester was the tribal capital of what we now call the East Midlands, and over the millennia has always been an important settlement on trade routes. It has also been the location for Parliament on a number of occasions, the first Parliament of England being at the now lost Leicester Cathedral in 1256AD under Henry III and then again in 1426 to crown the infant Henry IV. And, in keeping with the Henry theme, Henry VIII's fallen advisor Cardinal Thomas Wolsley died in Leicester Abbey on November 29, 1530, having been taken ill on his way to the Tower of London.

Industrialisation of the area was very quick, the region rapidly becoming a centre for industry and engineering that drew artisans and factory workers from far and wide. Serving this new population in the 19th Century was obviously important, and to that end one Henry Walker established a pork butcher's business there in 1880 on the high street, providing quality meat cuts to the hungry workers.

With the advent of World War II, meat rationing put a huge dent in the output of the factory, so the company was forced to consider alternatives. With potatoes in ample supply from the verdant soil, the factories slowly switched to producing hand-cut potato crisps, initially fried in your common or garden chip[1] fryer, and Walker's Crisps was born, giving Gary Lineker a retirement plan eighty years later. Leicester also became home to the National Space Centre in 2001, in part because of the University Of Leicester being one of the few places in the UK that has a department of Space Research (it was at this facility that the UK-controlled Beagle 2 Mars mission was conceived).

Leicester has a lot more to it, then, than meets the eye – although back in the early Nineties, for any kid growing up, it was a town full of possibilities but little else. In keeping with thousands of kids around the UK, and on the back of England's valiant showing in the 1990 World Cup held in Italy, the eleven-year-old Serge Pizzorno was obsessed with football in general, and particularly Leicester City. The youngster was, indeed, a talented player from an early age, bursting with potential, although his hometown club were slow off the mark in recognising his skill. So much so that he was forced to look elsewhere to continue his soccer education beyond that of the school playground, landing eventually at Nottingham Forest's academy, under the tutelage of the legendary Ian Storey-Moore. Despite the long history of Forest, it was something of a wrench for the Foxes-obsessed youngster, who nonetheless had a secret weapon designed to retain some part of loyalty to City.

"It was a strange one," Serge later confessed to interviewer Dean Jackson, "It was horrible 'cause Leicester City never really cared, but in my defence I used to wear Leicester City socks underneath my Forest socks when I played football, just to show I wasn't a traitor in any way. More fool Leicester, 'cause they should have noticed it, but they never did.[2]"

As an eleven and twelve-year-old, then, Serge was rubbing shoulders on the pitch with the likes of future England international, Jermaine Jenas, although at that age it is not always the most talented players who end up as professional soccerists. Life is all about discovery, and about having fun, and Pizzorno was certainly finding plenty of that. And not just on the football pitch.

"Around this area," says Andy Stone of fellow Leicester/Blaby-band-done-well, The Displacements, "there's a lot of creative people, people starting up bands. It's this little haven of [groups] starting to do well." One of the reasons for this is the nearby Community College in Countesthorpe, where Pizzorno hung out with fellow future collaborators, Tom Meighan and Chris Edwards.

"We were all into music," Sergio told the *Leicester Mercury*, "but they were only interested in you if you stayed behind for oboe lessons. And who, at 15, wants to do that?"[3] Well, oboeists, presumably.

Chris Edwards was born on December 20, 1980, and was drawn toward the creative side of matters at an early age. "My family is all-musical," he explained. "They all play instruments but they never really listened to a lot of music. I was into music at around eleven, buying records and listening to music. That's what I liked at the time."[4]

Music, however, is an immersive art-form as much as anything, and whilst listening to records is great, playing it is an even more satisfying experience. The young Edwards went for piano lessons, but soon, "quit them because the teacher was shit. My mum was a bit disappointed about that. I tried a lot of instruments before I started the guitar. I picked up the guitar when I was sixteen and loved it, so I carried on playing that. I then picked up the bass, played around a bit to see what I could do."[5]

Having met at school, Edwards and Pizzorno's shared love for music soon became apparent, folklore suggesting that a prototype mess-around band was in existence in the mid-Nineties, also featuring drummer Ben Kealy and a vocalist who happened to be Pizzorno's best mate at the time, jamming around at their shared educational establishment, Counteshope Community College.

It soon fizzled out, despite Serge's exhortations that, now the band was together, they would never have to work again. The original singer was soon history and, as luck – or fate – would have it, Tom Meighan, a mate of Serge and Chris from old, was soon to come on the scene as part of a growing gang of footy-loving, Oasis-inspired youngsters.

Blaby is a south Leicestershire town of around 6,000 inhabitants, originally established by Viking settlers and subsequently most famous for having the second oldest public house in the UK, *The Baker's Arms*, which was established in 1485. Come the 20th Century, and the small village was firmly entrenched as a satellite town of the larger conurbation of Leicester itself. Journalist Ben Cole grew up there.

"It's a really, really strange place," Cole told me. "Blaby is quite a run down area – but it's got a Waitrose! Chris and James [Jim Pratt] are quite important in Blaby folklore, because their dad ran the local carpet shop, and their uncles ran *Pratt Brothers*, a really famous shop in Blaby. *Everyone* knew where *Pratt Bros* was and when it shut down there was a real outcry … Blaby was the Pratt Brothers' town in those days."

Chris Pratt himself had met Tom Meighan, Chris Edwards and Sergio Pizzorno many times over the years, hanging out together in and out of school. "We were never musicians, we were just friends,[(6)]" explained Pizzorno. And that meant doing things that young men were wont to do, as Ben Cole recalls.

"They used to have this mate [who] they didn't want to hang around with – he was just one of those kids who was a bit annoying, [so] they filled this aftershave bottle with piss and left it for about two weeks. Eventually [he] used this piss aftershave!"

Tom Meighan was later to recall meeting the unique-looking Chris Pratt in the early days, remembering him for his sartorial style as much as anything else – at the time, Pratt was well-known for sporting rather impressive sideburns. Not only did he look cool, then, Pratt was also a well-known guitarist who'd already put his own prototype band together, having always been something of a free spirit. His earliest forays into music were between 1994 and 1997, playing a host of Oasis covers and Britpop classics just for the hell of it. But that individuality wasn't just down to the sideburns, as Cole recalls.

"He got this guitar for Christmas," laughs the childhood friend of the family. "It was a black Flying V, and it was weird 'cause around that time everyone was into either grunge or Britpop and having a Flying V was a bit out there. [He was] obviously ploughing [his] own furrow." Obviously.[(7)] But the local recreational park beckoned, an important part of the band's history according to Cole, who by the late Nineties was a journalist with the Nottingham-based music magazine, *City Lights*.

"I remember Sergio telling me that essentially how the band had come together was that they'd go for a smoke at this park in Blaby, and Tom'd start singing or shouting and over time they realised that what he was singing or shouting was quite good." And so Meighan slid nattily atop the previous singerless trio of Edwards, Pizzorno and Kealy for their debut gig, back in 1997.

"Chris Edwards' mum had decided to move to London," recalls Scott Gilbert, who at the time was running a studio in Leicester called Bedrock, "so they had a goodbye party, it was someone's birthday so they had this private party at Blaby Football Club. There was a disco in the corner and the lads turned up to play; this was their first gig … There was [nothing] there, absolutely nothing, just their guitar amps and the drum kit. They sat in the corner and we wired the vocals to go through the PA. [We] basically raided the disco bloke's kit to try and get a bit of volume for the band! It was absolutely amazing and they played about six or seven songs. Between every song they were spending two minutes or so tuning up and it was a right row! I remember saying to Chris, 'cause I like Chris, he's a fabulous young lad, I said, 'Ah, you'll have to stop doing that between your tracks, like, I've been in music for like ten years, and you don't do that, tell Serge not to tune his guitar between tracks 'cause it sounds bloody awful. Or at least turn your amp off!'"

Sage advice. The band's dubious debut performance also brought something very clearly to the fore: the four-piece needed an extra guitarist to bolster the line-up. And there could only be one choice – the Flying V must have swung it, and, in the best traditions of this sort of thing, the foursome cornered Chris Pratt in a local pub and asked him if he would like to join their band.

Happily Pratt replied in the affirmative – but from now he would be called Chris Karloff, please.[8]

CHAPTER TWO

Pass And Move

The quintet was now known as Saracuse. They were never the most active of live bands, however, although an early appearance (albeit only two of them) is recorded at Leicester's Shed on September 19, 1997, as Joe Betts of the venue recalls.

"That was really just an acoustic gig, just Tom and Serge," says Betts. "I'm roughly the same age, so I remember the bands who were around at that time and they were a decent acoustic duo. Fifty per cent of their set was classic Oasis songs: 'Live Forever', 'Supersonic', stuff like that. They didn't have much material. When they finally became a band and started gigging around as Saracuse, there were sort of three or four bands around at the time who were picked to possibly go all the way and they were one of them."[9] Nonetheless, having tasted the thrill of playing in front of a live audience, it was clear that music was, indeed, something that interested the group collectively and individually. "Even back then, they were doing gigs around the Midlands, [even though they] were quite young, only sixteen or seventeen," continues Betts, who quite reasonably notes that it must have been difficult for the nascent Saracuse to travel back and forth to gigs of their own volition anyway for more prosaic reasons. "It wasn't a case of being able to drive yourself to X, Y, Z [venues in different towns] but they were certainly active in the Midlands playing places in Wolverhampton, Dudley, Moseley, Nottingham. I remember seeing them at a gig in Loughborough in a small pub called The Three Nuns and from that gig they got picked up and got to play at Loughborough University, so it was a case of people recognising how good they were even back then, and as soon as they were old enough to get going they went out on their own and got gigs all over the place and just went for it."

Chris Edwards also, crucially, had met Scott Gilbert around 1996. Gilbert, now a successful photographer in Cambridge, is a jovial character whose recording business was going rather well at the time.

"Chris was still at school in Blaby and basically I was running a recording studio," Gilbert confirms. "We got bought out by the *Daily Mail* newspaper group at the time and started auditioning for voice-overs because we'd got into radio work. I met Chris' mum Angela and her now-husband Paul, and we helped them get their Equity cards through voice-over work and storybooks. At the same time, I met Chris – a young lad straight out of school – and he became my right-hand man. I was training him up to work in the studio alongside me." Those Ladybird kids' audio books, in fact, mark the debut recorded release of any future Kasabian member.

"Our scriptwriters used to sit there, get a little kids book and make it into an audio tape, script it and get all the effects. I'd send Chris to the audio library and he'd sit there for fucking hours pulling out all these CDs, sound effects of things you'd expect on kids' books. He'd whack them onto DAT and give it to me; I'd transfer it to the Mac and cut up the waveforms. We used to sit there putting all these things together and it was really good fun. So we were pretty much inseparable for three or four years."

"I have recordings of Chris being a mouse – we'd done these books for Ladybird and me and Chris were sitting there doing the voices then speeding the tape up, he was about 16 at the time. I've got all sorts of recordings, him singing on these things!"

As for Saracuse, they were concentrating on sorting out the wheat from the chaff, by now rehearsing up to four times a week and writing new material thick and fast, as well as having a lot of fun whilst they did it. "We had no real idea about what music we wanted to make at first," Serge offered. "It was very basic Beatles-y, Who-type numbers. We weren't trying to be cool, we just enjoyed jumping off each others' amps."[10] "We used to take a strobe light in with us, pretend that we were onstage."[11]

As for the other Chris – the newly monickered Karloff – the guitarist's life was taking a somewhat unexpected trajectory, the rather studious chap having eschewed the obvious route yet again. "Chris wasn't going away to college," a surprised Ben Cole recounts. "He was just working near to Blaby in this big storage place called Magner Park, it's one of those parks where loads of big businesses put their distribution centres. I think he worked for Asda as a packer. It was just a bit weird, it didn't add up. Probably everything about Chris at that time didn't add up, he drove a Volvo 340, a real old man's car." Big enough to carry around the group's gear, though, which was something of a boost given that most of 1997 and 1998 was spent getting ready to capture what turned out to be the debut recordings by Saracuse, entering Bedrock Studio in December, 1998 to lay down four tracks that are the basis from which everything was to subsequently emanate.

"By this time, Chris' mum had decided to move to London 'cause she got her Equity card," says the ever-helpful Scott Gilbert. "I remember it ever so well. He'd just got the band together and I said, 'Get the band in, let's do a demo,' so they all come in, they plugged in, we mic'd up and did it live, we multi-tracked it and they recorded four songs, it sounded like bad Stereophonics sort-of tracks. They rattled through the material. Everyone else had gone home so I stayed behind and [did] this demo for them."

Those four tracks are an interesting insight into the songwriting skill of the band at the time. The session begins with 'What's Going On', the tom-toms are heavy, with a rather slinky, bluesy guitar lick from Karloff playing off Meighan's lyrics about staying up all night talking, cheap thrills and finally, triumphantly, breaking free to sunnier climes. [12] Prophetic indeed. It's certainly not related to the track of the same name made famous by Marvin Gaye. 'Interlude' is a rather quaint, silly but skilled thirty seconds of Rhodes keyboard played by drummer Ben Kealy. Then there's the tom-tom heavy 'Life Of Luxury', [13] an indie rock track that takes a very Stereophonics-esque ambience, marries it to a traditional storytelling template and applies it to Saracuse's own interpretation of friendship. The anthemic 'Shine On' is a call-to-arms acoustic-based ditty that could easily have been an out-take from *Be Here Now* (if not quite of the standard of *Definitely Maybe*). In satisfyingly memorable rock tradition, the demo CD was presented to the band on Christmas Eve, 1999[14]. In truth, it's a slightly cheesy set of tracks that, whilst proficient, is nothing more than a snapshot of the strong musical influences and – in the case of the false ending then singalong coda of 'Life Of Luxury' – an early sign of the crowd-pleasing bent of the group as well as their growing flair for songwriting and arrangement. "We multi-tracked with the vocals in one take," recalls Scott Gilbert, "then mixed it down as best we could on Christmas Eve just before we finished work."

It was also to bring them into contact with a more professional side of the music industry, according to Gilbert. "Those tracks they then played to Alan Rawlings, who was their first manager," says the producer.

Saracuse were starting to draw attention to their activities by this point, with a host of local journalists sniffing around them, including old sparring partner Ben Cole of *City Lights* magazine, who had been keeping in touch with the group's activities through his contacts with Chris Pratt/Karloff and his older brother, James (who was often known also as Jim).

"Part of the reason I went to see them was that all of the kids who I was really scared of at school were suddenly going to see this band," Ben laughs. "There was a famous gig, not in Leicester but somewhere nearby, where a guy had had a massive fight with somebody in the place whilst they were playing so I thought to myself, 'Right I've gotta see this, even if the band's crap I'm gonna see a load of people from my school days which could be very funny.'"

According to most of the received wisdom of the genesis of the group, one of these very early gigs was in The Princess Charlotte, another of Leicester's dedicated music venues. It is, when busy, capable of generating a rather special atmosphere, the kind of place where you see the rising stars of the music scene as they are on the verge of breaking through (or otherwise). As such, it is something of an acid test for new bands: to pack out and rock out the Charlotte is no small deal; it is where Cole went to see Saracuse in 1999.

"Chris was still playing the black Flying V – it was kind of an understated Flying V!" he laughs. "It's part of Chris, I guess, having a Flying V; you'd expect him to be the lead guitarist, foot on the monitor and all that sort of stuff, but the very first thing that was really obvious was that you couldn't see him onstage – he was kind of hidden behind all the amps! But you could work out that the good stuff wasn't coming from anyone else, it was coming from him at that point. Tom was onstage in the Liam Gallagher, big furry coat, just standing exactly like Liam. I don't know if they did an Oasis cover or not but they might as well have done 'cause it was just really plodding sort of Oasis-lite."

The repertoire of the group at this embryonic stage was mostly inspired by the attitude and the music of groups like that. Make no mistake, Saracuse was a gang, and much like the tightness of the Gallagher brothers and their crew, it was a case of fit in, or ship out, as the original mess-around singer had found out to his cost a couple of years earlier. This was soon to cause a few more problems, but for now the band's occasional gigs (another is recorded at The Shed on September 22, 1999) were raucously received by a mixture of old schoolmates and new fans. Saracuse were also starting to write some accomplished songs amidst the more obviously referential stuff.

"They did all these kind of lame Oasis covers," sighs Cole, before brightening up at another memory of the band also "playing this fantastic song which had this arpeggiated guitar, which I'm sure was one written by Chris [Karloff], it was called 'Charlie' and it was just amazing. I was blown away 'cause I'd effectively seen two bands: this one boring band and the other band doing this one fantastic song. I remember writing the review for *City Lights* and it was something like, 'Just write more songs like this one 'cause the rest of it's not really that great.'"

That track, also known as 'Angels', was recorded at Bedrock during the band's second studio outing, in 1999. It is miles ahead of anything that Saracuse had previously written, 'Shine On' possibly excepted, and certainly the high point of the six tracks laid down during that particular session. The other tracks were all originals: 'Highest Number' a rather forgettable rocker built round an Edwards bass-line and revealing the group's fixation on The Who. 'Ten Past Three' is a tuneful workout where Meighan wonders what he's doing and where he's headed, with a catchy chorus about sleeping on the wind, whilst 'In And Out Satellite' starts with Serge giggling at something the band are clearly amused with before they launch into a track that clearly references The Beatles' 'Lucy In The Sky With Diamonds'. 'Dirty Dishes' is a love/hate song to a cook named Mary that, alarmingly, sounds a little like the music good ol' Robbie Williams was hearing in his head when he was hanging round Oasis, just before they got bored of him and started calling him funny things like, 'the fat dancer from Take That'. There's also an acoustic version of 'Waiting For You Now'.

A third studio session swiftly followed, a mixture of full band tracks and acoustic sketches. "They were still finding themselves," muses producer Scott Gilbert. "When you listen to the acoustic stuff, it's just Serge sitting there by himself, writing."

'The Federation' reveals again the me-and-you-against-the-world thread to the band's outlook, on one hand fighting the influence of shadowy forces at work, whilst concurrently hoping that friendship will carry them home. 'The Warrior', by contrast, is an odd mix of a paean to John & Yoko but featuring a distinctly Jamaican-tinged chorus. It's a good-natured vibe all round, but musically rather a strange collision. Still, The Beatles themselves were always fans of all manner of not only lyrical but also musical pastiche, so a little exploration was more or less expected. And for a band trying to find their feet, looking at The Beatles for inspiration ain't such a bad thing. Tom and Serge also seem like they're having so much fun that it's churlish to say anything else, so I shall refrain. There are also run-throughs of 'Come Back Down', a new song which holds within it both melody and the pilot light for a much more fiery effort later down the line, the very introspective 'Just Relax', 'Keep It Safe' and 'Sniffing Glue', on which Tom sounds the most Liam-like he ever had done on tape.

Full band tracks include the rocktastic, distorto-vocalled stomper 'Pump It Up' (no relation to the Elvis Costello classic), the extremely Oasis-like 'Excuse To Get Wasted' which is an ode to the strength of friends and how legendary they can be, pulling each other through trouble and good times alike. Then there's 'Get Around' a knock-off indie rocker about not being tied down in a relationship, 'Stupid, Nothing Matters' a rather more downbeat workout that deals with the aftermath of an argument, whilst holding within it the hope of love, and 'You Won't Forget Me' which is the full version of the previous session's 'Waiting For You Now'. This session was more of the same, in all honesty, notable for the acoustic rough demos as much as the general themes of the material which are, more or less without exception, about finding answers and searching for a satisfying place in this confusing world of lost love, panic, and occasional magic.

"You can really hear the musicianship in them," offers Scott Gilbert. "You can really hear that the band are tight. It kinda surprised me 'cause none of them really said a lot, apart for Tom. Serge was really head down, the drummer just didn't really communicate much and Chris was dead quiet anyway. Tom was kind of in-your-face. You'd sort of turn up to do some tracks, you'd think they were lads just fucking about then they'd do these live tracks and it's really, really good. Really tight. Okay, there's bits that they wouldn't do now, but you can really hear that they could actually play whereas the first session just sounds like four lads had got together, picked up someone's CD and just [sounded like that]."

Whilst the group was still finding its feet, the tight songwriting of groups like Stereophonics, Oasis and, of course, The Beatles, was still a major influence. Everyone has to start somewhere, and the period between 1998 and 1999 was spent mainly refining their craft as a band, and learning more about the possibilities of the studio itself.

"Around the time we were spending a bit more [effort] on production, getting the right vocal sounds," says Scott Gilbert. "When I listen to it back-to-back, I can tell when we were fucking around with different vocal distortions and all that kind of stuff. The performances were great; they just sort of plugged in and then me and Chris Edwards would do the mix-downs on our dinner breaks, 'cause he was working for me at the studio so we'd say, 'Oh, let's just do that mix for a couple of hours', you know?"

The band freely admitted that the early days were not entirely spent seriously up to a point, but nonetheless they were fully committed to proceedings. "It was our religion when we were young," Chris Edwards was to later admit. "Instead of going to other things like other people did, we used to do band practice four times a week."[15]

Whilst the group busied themselves with rehearsing, recording and the occasional gig, the manager Alan Rawlings was hawking the demos around to contacts within the music industry, and generally doing what managers do, as Scott Gilbert recalls from his own experiences at that (in)famous Charlotte appearance.

"They did their first gig in The Charlotte, well, it wasn't the first gig – it was the first gig in Leicester outside of a family birthday party! Rawlings actually paid me sixty quid to go there for the night and sound engineer it. He asked me to record it onto MiniDisc so I have their first concert archived, the first time they played the Charlotte."

The engineer also clears up an incident that happened at that particular gig that led to Saracuse being banned from one of the city's key venues. It's something that has largely passed into folklore as being down to youthful high spirits, but the facts are that a confrontation did take place at the gig, although again, contrary to popular belief, it wasn't necessarily of the band's design.

"They actually say, 'Yeah, there was a fight and we got banned,' and it's dead true but .. they were supporting another band that caused the fight, but [Saracuse] got the blame for some reason! I swear to God it wasn't the lads who were causing the argument or the fight, it was the band they were playing with! ... It was the main band who were fighting! But for some reason Saracuse got the blame."

Whoever was responsible, it never does any great harm for groups to be associated with what you might call rock 'n' roll behaviour; as the new millennium dawned, Saracuse's increased work ethic began to be allied to another set of musical influences altogether. Both factors were to produce some stunning results, for good and for bad.

CHAPTER THREE

Offside

2000 in Leicester would begin with an event intended to celebrate the area's music and musicians, nattily entitled 'Red Leicester' and set for February 26, 2000. It was Chris 'Dibs' Edwards' employers at Bedrock Studios who had the idea to bring together the cream of the local acts at the time for an all-day concert, to take place at the city's cavernous DeMontford Hall. Artists including The Wrinkly Pink Catsuits (particular favourites of the Saracuse boys at the time), A.K.A.Weave (who featured Kav Sandhu, later to become part of Happy Mondays), Last Man Standing, The Incurables and a host of other Leicester-based bands were added to a frantic ten hours of musical goodness. Flyers and posters were hastily put together, featuring Saracuse quite high up the bill.

At this stage, thanks to having been banned from the Charlotte, Saracuse were rather less than visible on the live scene, London-based management or not. The DeMontford event was to celebrate the talent in the area, and whatever the future held, in a sense nobody – or everybody – was a superstar on the day. Unfortunately, a disagreement over dressing rooms meant that the band never actually played the 'Red Leicester' event, which was a great shame.

If the group themselves were disappointed by their non-appearance at this one-off, special event, they were also a little downbeat when the associated triple CD was released, simply entitled *Red* and put out by Bedrock to celebrate nearly ten years of recording bands in the area. Comprising two audio CDs of thirty-six tracks by thirty-six different bands, and a bonus CD-Rom disk of some 155 MP3s, there was plenty of space with which to play around. Saracuse, despite their relative lack of profile, were obvious candidates for inclusion, not just because of Chris Edwards' band having been recorded in Bedrock downtime, but also because he'd been tape operator, or engineer, for a large number of the sessions from which the CD tracks are culled.

"Alan Rawlings didn't want us to put what he called a 'Major Track' on the main CD," recalls Gilbert. "He wanted us to have an acoustic track and we were like, 'We're not doing that. We've only got room for eighteen bands to have one song each, thirty six bands on two discs, we're not gonna put an acoustic track on the main CD.'" So they didn't and Saracuse were thus destined to never release anything commercially. The new millennium had kicked in, but here was a group who couldn't play the main venue of their hometown after some trouble they didn't start, and had now missed out on a high profile local event and CD.

However, musically, the semi-enforced absence from the 'scene' had its benefits. With the band now congregating round Chris Edwards' mother's then-boyfriend's old house in Fosse Lane, there was plenty of time to listen to other kinds of music, as well as explore technological possibilities even further. Working on a PC set-up with early versions of recording software like Cubase and the drum loop program Acid, the band began to lay down more experimental work built round their growing interest in other genres including Can, Tangerine Dream, Blackilicious and Beastie Boys. A favourite at the time in Fosse Lane was the 1998 Boards Of Canada album, *Music Has The Right To Children*, which melded together an indie sensibility with judicious use of samples, sourced sounds and a whole lot of synths.

Returning to Bedrock studio on September 21, 2000, Saracuse continued largely to plough the epic, indie-rock furrow that had marked their career, such as it was, to date. A funky version of 'Come Back Down' was recorded, the track still going through permutations and stylistic tinkering, the band clearly still playing with the different possibilities engendered within the basic rawness of the acoustic version; also in this session, a remixed version appeared featuring a rather interesting bell-like sample loop (which was included on a CD of loops and samples that Scott Gilbert had installed on the Fosse Lane PC), a loop that was later to resurface in a rather different, and massively more famous, form … more of which in due course.

"I was always throwing drum loops at them. [They were always] making little breakbeats and that. It were great: 'Here's some studio time', they had a PC and it was, 'Here's some software' and that's sort of how they got creative and that was obviously Tom and Serge."

In contrast to the electronic exploration, 'Some Fingz In My Jeans' is a fairly straightforward rocker which had the group's manager tearing his hair out at Tom's pronunciation. "I remember Alan Rawlings saying to Tom, 'It's not FINGS, it's THINGS'," laughs Gilbert … I remember saying to Tom, 'Fucking hell, man, that's how you sing, you're from Leicester.' And you know what he's like, in your face all the time, 'Yeah know whatya mean Scott, wicked, wicked, yeah!' But you can really hear Tom's style, even on the demos, it's amazing stuff." Indeed it is, and the band are certainly ramping it up towards full flow in this session. 'Somewhere Nowhere', 'Sun Ain't Gonna Shine' and the full-band version (and therefore the definitive recorded version), of the confident and very catchy, 'Wait For You Now' are dashed off almost insouciantly by a band, a *gang*, that was absolutely together on their new four-rehearsals-a-week focus. The other track featuring the full band is a very interesting one indeed, known here as 'Rain', a plaintive, soaring melody that swirls and reaches for answers. Again, this track (also called 'Rain In My Soul' elsewhere) would hold within it the earliest elements for an entirely different track some years later. In this session, two demo tracks were laid down whilst the group waited for Kealy to rattle up one day.

"The drummer was always good, always held the band together," concedes Gilbert. "I didn't really speak to him much, he never really said much, he was always sat at the back with his girlfriend, and was [often] the last person there. Me and Chris Edwards would mic the drums up before he'd turn up then there'd be some acoustic tracks recorded to pass the time." It was at this session that 'Same Old Story' (a typical Saracuse track, full of melody, regret and hope in one indie rock package) and 'Lost Soul' were recorded. As Serge Pizzorno sings the latter, the lyrics flirt with the concept that music is his soul, but he feels lost, the very atmosphere is intimately drawn toward his dilemma. The theme would be returned to again and again, the title recycled for a completely new piece of music, and the track, albeit with a different name entirely, would resurface in a very similar form years later and become something of a calling card and a call to arms.

However, this was to be the last session that Saracuse were to record in their hometown's Bedrock Studios. Scott Gilbert philosophises as to his part in the band's development and how the band members themselves came across.

"Tom was the one that's kind of in-your-face ... Tom's really absolutely hyper, as he's talking to you his nose is up touching yours in a kind of friendly, mad kind of way! But it's just the energy he's got, the same energy he's got onstage. And Serge is the same Serge, you know, head down, don't say a lot ... just the same energy [though]. They were sat in the studio once waiting for the drummer, I just flicked on record straight to DAT and Serge was writing songs [on the spot]. Tom and Serge work together so well, literally Serge will come up with an idea singing it and Tom would come in over the top putting his own idea over it, and there were all these little things, little gems materialising before your eyes.

I think these demos represent five lads getting together, all from the same area. I didn't even know Chris Edwards played bass and the next thing he was playing in this band, and they just developed. You can hear it over a very short period, even over a year and a half, the development is from ripping off Stereophonics and trying to do psychedelic funky stuff but all the time, throughout all these sessions, you've got Serge sitting down playing acoustic guitar and just coming up with all these melodies and ideas so all these things are being born in the studio."

By this stage, Ben Cole was an established reporter on the music scene, his reviews and interviews a major part of *City Lights* magazine, which was based in Sergio's old hoofing ground of Nottingham. He recalls interviewing Saracuse around the time of the fourth studio session.

"It was really weird [interviewing them] 'cause Tom was really how I expected meeting Liam Gallagher to be, really in your face," laughs Cole. "He kept saying their sound was 'Trip Pop' which he was really proud of, really pleased he'd come up with this way of describing what they did. It wasn't really the best description! At the time they were really different to the rest of the bands in Leicester who were fey indie types – they were this gang. The first gig, with Chris playing the Flying V, this lad called Jarred came along and he was doing backflips and goading people into responding to this band. There was something very different about them."

The band also managed to be 'unbanned' from The Charlotte, performing there once more with a much tighter sound and a set of much, much better songs. Cole was in the audience, of course, and it was a gig that showed just how far the quintet had come in the intervening period.

"It was late 2000, and they played the Princess Charlotte again and it was like this interesting band had started to take shape. Whilst at the first gig, Tom had been Liam Gallagher; he seemed like Michael Stipe this time ... like something bad had happened to him, he'd had some sort of knock to his confidence ... like something really major had happened in his life. He seemed to be being far more introspective in his performance; he was doing all the crouching, putting his hand in front of his face and things like that and that with the quite laddish music behind it suddenly made it really, really interesting. And they certainly had been writing more songs like 'Charlie', there were loads more like that. They were playing a version of 'Rain On My Soul'. I remember Serge singing, 'cause he hadn't sung the first time they'd played, and then they did this fantastic thing at the end. The band seemed really *together*. They got a DJ up on stage and I thought, 'Uh-oh, this is gonna be *terrible*' 'cause they were saying they'd not rehearsed it. But it was absolutely amazing, just really really cool. Afterwards they were saying, 'We realised we need to be more interesting than just Oasis.' Something had definitely happened to Tom, he really had changed his outlook on things and he told me he'd been listening to his mum's soul records. I remember that was his response."That DJ was one Daniel Ralph Martin, a friend of the band and soon to play a larger part in the tale as a whole.

There were big changes afoot in many ways: not only were the musical influences broader, Chris Dibs changed his job at this time too, with Mike at Bedrock's insistence that as Chris now had a manager for his band, there would be no more free studio time for Saracuse.

"Chris then left and worked for a telephone engineer," reveals Scott Gilbert. "I said to Chris, 'I know you're in a band, you enjoy it and that but you've got an opportunity here to be a telephone engineer and you can do the studio part-time. Don't put all your money on being a rock star, 'cause it ain't gonna happen!' Seriously, I was kind of letting him down gently, know what I mean? I hope he didn't think I was being [defeatist], I just cared for the man ...[16]'

The band weren't always prone to making good decisions, however, and though Karloff's Flying V may have been mothballed by this point, Scott Gilbert recalls 'fondly' a set of instruments that really should have remained in the shop.

"I remember they all bought guitars by Dane. Bloody awful guitars they were. The original ones were these vintage Fifties and Sixties guitars, but they had a reissue back in about 1999/2000 and they were like bits of balsa wood. The Beatles had Rickenbackers, so they thought they'd use Danes. Chris had an aqua blue bass, it looked awful and it sounded awful as well!"

The other major change in proceedings was also imminent – a change of drummer. "The drummer at the time really stuck out like a sore thumb," offers Ben Cole, because "the rest of them were either really Oasis-looking or really long-haired. There was something going on with them but he was like earrings, cap ... it was part of that gang mentality thing, he was sort of in the gang then they went off in one direction and he went in a completely different direction. Basically, Chris Karloff's story was that the drummer had gone off and bought this really fast Audi and the rest of the band were like, 'We're not into that, that's nothing to do with us'. So they'd kind of parted [ways]." [(17)]

"It was hard," Tom Meighan later recounted, "because [Ben] was our friend, but he was out boy racing all the time... only interested in the size of his exhaust pipe or the sub in the boot."[(18)]

Another intriguing take on the tale is provided by one Ash Hanning, who was the in-house sound engineer at Leicester's Sumo and the nearby Coventry Coliseum venues. Hanning recalls mixing the band live a number of times in the Saracuse days, and remembers Kealy as being still with the band who were now beginning to draw some record company attention of their own. During this phase, Ben parted company with the band and Hanning suggests various outside influences were involved – the implication perhaps being a record company.

"Playing-wise he was fantastic, it wasn't anything complicated but it didn't need to be 'cause a lot of the tribal beats were on backing tracks as well as being played live with the samples going. You didn't need any fancy stuff, it was just to give it drive and a bit of balls. But he was told [he was no longer part of the band]. It was harder 'cause he'd been with them from school, his very first band, he'd been right there from day one so it was really difficult 'cause he was their really good mate."

As ever with such matters, there are several shades of opinion as to the precise nature of the drummer's departure, and Hanning's take on the tale places Kealy still with the group as late as 2002, which is at odds with most of the received wisdom from other sources which all point to 2001 as Zero Year. Regardless, the facts were that Ben Kealy (who, in keeping with most of the rest of the gang, had a slightly inexplicable nickname, 'Deggers') was no longer a part of the group, of the gang. Saracuse's story really ends with the departure of Kealy, and the remaining members were therefore kicked even further towards the loops, samples and beat processing techniques that they were beginning to hold so dear.

CHAPTER FOUR

Pre-Season Training

With the departure of Kealy, the group could easily have jacked it in, but there was a collective growing interest in more interesting music and technological possibilities, one being that a drumloop on a DAT tape could serve just as well as a human for the music the band was creating (for now at least). With Serge bringing in the pennies at his job with Allied Domecq, working in the warehouse, and Tom Meighan gainfully employed by Dr. Martens, the group were also able to have more than a few great nights out to celebrate life and freedom in all its facets, listening to Primal Scream and watching the Spaghetti Westerns of Sergio Leone, including the *Fistful Of Dollars* trilogy. The new music was coming thick and fast, but this time the prolific Pizzorno and the imaginative Karloff were finding much interest in colliding the acoustic framework within sequenced electronica, whilst adding effects and messing around. The possibilities were truly endless, and though the band were now no longer recording at Bedrock, the PC was ever-ready to handle the sketches and ideas at any time of the day or night.

Neil Ridley was a musician around the area in the late Nineties and early years of the new millennium, and recalls that Saracuse had by this point also come to the decision that perhaps incubation of their ideas outside their hometown was a route worth exploring, live-wise at least.

"I sensed from them that they didn't want to be that band that just broke locally, [or just] enjoyed the fact that they were local faces, you know?" he explained in an interview for this book. "To them that wasn't important. What was important to them was the fact that they were getting about doing what they were doing. That it was a little bit different-sounding." Not without some belief in their own ability, too, however.

"They'd be supporting bands who came into town and we'd go along. I remember Tom, standing in the audience watching, immediately railing against one of these bands going, 'You're shit!' and immediately knowing that he had that confidence that frontmen seldom have."[19]

With the focus firmly outside Leicester for the time being, the band were more often than not down in London, where their management was based. Whilst there, they'd randomly got chatting with a particular music store owner who would often lend them pieces of equipment for gigs and the like, and the relationship expanded into discussing the studio dilemma. The store owner immediately raised an eyebrow, beckoned the lads in closer and whisper-tipped the band off about a studio that was well-regarded in rock circles. If Saracuse's ears pricked up at that, the deciding factor was that none other than Noel Gallagher was known to rate the facility highly and often nipped away there himself to lay down demo tracks. Its location? Bristol. Saracuse made a mental note of it for future use and subsequently went back to doing what they did best, and that was exploring the endless swirls and splendours of music in all its myriad forms.

"In the early days," continues Neil Ridley, "[I think] it was Serge and Chris Pratt that were really shaping the sounds. Serge is a bit more studied I think, one of the things he's always had is that ability to translate the ideas really well. I knew Chris better than the other guys at the time, we share some kind of uncle or second uncle removed somewhere, anyway he'd come round to mine and we'd talk about Korg MS-20s and analogue keyboards and all that sort of stuff. It was obvious that he had a real love of doing something different; he was particularly into vintage analogue film soundtracks. We often joked about Wendy Carlos who used to be Walter Carlos, the guy who wrote the soundtrack to *A Clockwork Orange*. Stuff like that. There was often a running joke about the synth soundtracks that used to be going on, back in the day, we thought they were as contemporary then as they are now."

Chris Pratt/Karloff and Ridley's chats would get almost esoteric at times, with a breadth of influences that reached into some very interesting areas of some of the most seminal music concrete artistes and tape-loop pioneers who had worked in the nether reaches of music and audio manipulation over the years.

"We often used to talk about the BBC Radiophonic Workshop [famous for the Dr. Who theme] and how they used to really, without any use of modern technology, create and craft these amazing things from everyday sounds; there was that element of real pushing of boundaries, and certainly pushing the limits of technology. It took a great deal of time and skill, they had to spend ages putting these things together. And that was kind of the way he wanted to approach things. The first thing that struck me was that he definitely had that desire to create something different and not think the same as other bands, certainly."

So much so that Karloff, whilst not with Saracuse, was more often than not to be found messing about in a group with his brother, Jim, the wonderfully-monikered More Monkey Than Man, as Ben Cole recalls.

"Basically they were taking computers to bits and sticking forks in them to see what kind of sounds came out, that sort of thing! I'd acquired from my then-employers some funny old vintage keyboards and one was a Suzuki Omnichord so I said to Chris, 'Have this, see what you can make out of this.' I'd been using it for a bit and I had two so I gave them one, I think I gave them a Bentley Rhythm Ace [vintage drum machine] as well." Two more pieces of equipment to hook up to the Fosse Lane PC set-up, and two more bits of gear to play with. Flashing lights! Buttons! *I wonder what happens if I press this…*

The group had, as individuals, grown up with the twin spectres of the grunge scene as led by the introspective Kurt Cobain of Nirvana, and the anti-establishment rave scene of the late Eighties. Add into the mix the attitude and soccer-terrace street-smarts of Oasis, plus a little of the electronic beat-dirt of Primal Scream, frame it all with the more experimental and esoteric music concrete techniques of the BBC Radiophonic Workshop and the nihilism of the Italian Futurist Movement, and you're pretty close to what was swirling around in the creative air as Saracuse began to morph into something else entirely.

"When we started, we wanted to sound like Lennon and McCartney," Serge was to later explain to interviewer Matt Cartmell. "And then you get deeper and deeper into it and you realise that doesn't help anyone because it's been done, so we got a computer and started doing it all ourselves. Making beats and [so on]. The deeper and deeper we fell into listening to vast amount of music, when we first started it was, there was a few bands you listened to, and then as you get into it more, loads more bands come in and you're like, 'Fucking hell, that's really good'. And you know, like a tree, it keeps splintering off. But it was just to make a good tune, and then make it interesting. Like in the Sixties, for instance [the Beatles track] 'Tomorrow Never Knows' is a fucking awesome tune. Then everything that's built around it [in the arrangement and the musical context] makes it sound different and fresh."

The rave scene was based around a collective wish to keep the party going outside the designated hours, venues and headspaces of The Establishment during the mid-to-late Eighties. It's hard to envisage it now, but there was a time when the height of rebellion was the wearing of a fluorescent, smiley face T-shirt and heading out in convoy to secret locations in the middle of the night to dance 'til dawn, pot of Vick's Vaporub in your back pocket for a 5.30am boost. It truly was a very odd time, the government truly running scared, the tabloids and broadsheets were full of scare stories that essentially boiled down to the fact that *Drugs Are Bad, Okay?*[20]. Tragic though some of those terrible tales undoubtedly were, it was and is a continuing tragedy that the subsequent Criminal Justice Act was brought in, effectively making impromptu gatherings of like-minded individuals illegal. Steps were taken, of course, and very sensibly too, to attempt to educate the younger generation as to how to recognise certain substances if offered them, as Serge recalled.

"[We were] very aware [of drugs]. Policemen would be coming in with their open boxes with like a plastic cover over with all the drugs in: 'Don't touch this', and you knew, you'd already seen it … we walked around school with those T-shirts with fucking 'Just add L.S.D.' and 'E Tops' [written on them], not really knowing what it meant totally. But you knew it was bad so you'd do it." A very familiar response, and rather an inevitable one. Everyone surely must know that the best way to get a teenager to do something is to forbid it[21]. Governments aside, of course. But the group was drawn toward the outlaw element of the scene, even if they didn't fully understand what exactly all of the implications might be.

"[Although] we went down the football, we were more ravers," continued Serge. "We were too young to go [to the raves], but we preferred [that scene to the grunge scene]. It was a bit more dangerous, you know. It was like you couldn't buy it from HMV and you'd never see it on telly so you'd just have to borrow tapes off mates and then the older kids who would hang around the parks or whatever would give you these fucking tapes. We knew they were all doing Es and that. It was glamourised."

Back in the Kasabian camp, however, and the sonic side was starting to take shape, as Serge was to explain to the legendary Irish journalist, Hannah Hamilton. "DJ Shadow opened a lot of doors for us," he smiled. "Then we found the Warp label (Aphex Twin, Boards of Canada, Squarepusher, Nightmares On Wax). Anything from there, even if you didn't like it, gave you ideas. I think what electronica always lacked though was a bit of soul, a bit of rawness. And these days, rock 'n' roll lacks imagination, so to be able to put the two genres together is quite interesting."

And now, more than ever, the group was stretching its wings out to begin to do just that. Despite, or perhaps because of, the fact that they were drummerless, by the time that the next studio session, at Bink Bonk[22] Studios, was scheduled, the musical focus was absolutely more interesting. One new track in particular was to prove absolutely pivotal in the group's career, and it is a track without which this book would stop here.[23]

CHAPTER FIVE

Sample It, Loop It, Fuck It And Eat It.

Saracuse decamped to Bristol for a very swift session at Bink Bonk, under the watchful eye of producer Mat Sampson, well-known on the Bristol scene (and further afield) for his mastery of the equipment, and also for having many contacts within the live scene of the area. During a brief few hours of recording, Saracuse were also to hook up with a session drummer by the name of Ian Matthews, who was extremely well-known and respected on the jazz and trip-hop scene. He was also a full-time member of the Virgin-signed trip-hop act Ilya, which would have pleased Tom Meighan's 'trip-pop' fixation immensely. For now, however, the effectively drummerless quartet were more interested in laying down their constantly-being-refined tracks. There was another incarnation of 'Rain On My Soul' as well as a new ditty that subsequently became called 'Beneficial Herbs'. However, most notably there was a groove-based track which was, unusually, not based around the rhythm and timbre of the acoustic guitar but was rather more reliant on a sequenced, atmospheric soundscape. It could have come, in fact, from the Stone Roses' darker moments in the *Second Coming* sessions or even the Happy Mondays, although it featured some odd noises and samples that those Manchester boys would never have countenanced. And although the drums were recorded live, the song, even in this prototype form, held within it a huge amount of promise as to what it was to become.

The title of this hyperspatial groove?

'Processed Beats'.

This pivotal song is a *Galaxian* leap from the days of sub-Stereophonics workthroughs, and Ben Cole for one was at last getting his hands on genuinely fascinating material from the 'interesting band' he'd first been intrigued by some two years previously.

"I was asking Chris Karloff for a demo for ages," he says, "cause I'd seen them twice and thought they were really good. I was just asking him for a demo for ages, and ages, and ages. He said, 'We've not been in the studio, we've not done this, we've not done that' and then [eventually] he said, 'We're down in Bristol' [recording one]."

Later that year, one fateful Sunday around Christmas 2001, recalls Cole, Karloff came round to drop the results off on a CD. Cole, having over-indulged the night before, was in bed and decided at last to have a listen to what his mate's brother's band sounded like with some sequenced stuff – and, of course, the infamous Omnichord – to play with.

"I remember putting the demo on – the house was one of the Gas Houses that are famous in Leicester, a three storey house. I had a huge stereo in the bedroom on the third floor and I was lying there, I was in a bit of a mess from the Saturday night. I put it on and the first track was 'Processed Beats' and I remember sitting up and saying, out loud, 'I just didn't expect that.' It was incredible. Then 'Rain On My Soul' was alright and 'Beneficial Herbs' was incredible and I thought, 'This is a band who are going to go miles 'cause they are just incredible.'"

By this time, Neil Ridley had pretty much moved on from performing to becoming a scout for Sony BMG, a job that basically entails going to lots of gigs and tracking the progress of the very best groups of the area, and then reporting the findings to the A&R staff at the record label whose job it is to take the advice of their regional scouts into account when reporting in turn to their bosses who may make the decision to sign a band to a record contract. It's a simple hierarchy on paper, but in practice the roles are often blurred. Ridley himself would rely in part on tip-offs from his local contacts in magazines, promoters and studio staff alike but fundamentally what it requires is good ears for music, a bit of patience, and one hell of a lot of passion. The regional scouts are quite often unpaid, looking not necessarily to further their own careers but more to give a leg-up to talented artists under their jurisdiction in the music industry. It is also true, of course, that recommending subsequently successful bands is hardly going to be to the detriment of an A&R scout's career, so the relationship is essentially symbiotic. The music industry comes in for masses of stick, at times rightly so, but in essence it is these scouts, who brave rain, wind, hail and thousands of shite bands night after night, who are often the very first to spot the rough ear-kissing diamonds amidst the honking, rehashed sonic effluent.

And when Neil Ridley finally got his hands on the demo, he too was bowled over and rushed in to the office of his boss, David Field. "I thought it was amazing," recalls Cole. "I played it to the head of A&R at the time, and he said, 'Wow, how do you know about this? We're planning to sign these guys!' And I kind of ended up getting a job indirectly out of it 'cause I guess I kind of knew them but it wasn't like I signed or A&Rd them 'cause they were a long way into that process. It felt like a nice thing for Leicester, that I was doing okay and the band was doing great as well."

Things weren't quite so straightforward as all that, however, with the label themselves trying out a rather different style of approaching the concept of signing bands up. Uniquely, A&R Director Nick Raymonde had in previous incarnations been both a heavy metal producer, run a metal label called Kamaflage – and been heavily responsible for the career of Take That prior to being charged to become part of Sony BMG's new 'cool' rock label. And the structure of the label, and the subsequent atmosphere created by a small and vibrant team all pulling in the same direction, was to ultimately be massively beneficial to Saracuse's subsequent success.

"The scouts would basically bring the things in," explains the often-hilariously funny Raymonde. "The chain of command there was quite flat actually, at the same time that they would report to me, there was really no distinction between myself, [Head of A&R] Ged Doherty or even a marketing or promotions person. They'd bring it in but let Ged hear the stuff at the same time as they'd let me hear it, so that was good and when I went to talk to Ged about a band he'd already know about it 'cause he'd listen to everything everybody had. So he was already aware of a lot of groups in that showcase that day, and that was how it worked. There were four or five A&R people at my level where you were making records and signing bands, but you still needed to get the approval of Ged and ultimately you still needed to have a sense within the record label that people really wanted you to sign the band. You weren't flying solo on it; you needed to make sure that the promotions and marketing people had seen it."

In order to further sort out the wheat from the chaff, a series of band showcases were to be set up, with ten or so groups all having the opportunity to play in front of the record label staff and show off their wares. Showcases like this are not unusual in the music industry, although quite often they take place in the band's rehearsal rooms or a recording studio. Even The Beatles did it, auditioning with George Martin who was more intrigued by the humour of this gang from the north of England than enamoured with the music at the time, and we all know what happened there.

Unbeknownst to Ridley, a scout by the name of Darren Dixon had already tipped BMG off about the Blaby boys (thanks in part to manager Alan Rawlings sending around of the Bink Bonk demos), and so it was that Saracuse travelled to Putney to set up and face down whatever fate had in store for them.

"We did some auditions," confirms Raymonde. "We'd never done this before, it was Ged Doherty's idea. I had four scouts working for me and the idea was that they'd basically bring all the acts that they were interested in, and considering getting involved with, acts they were wanting to sign – getting them all into a rehearsal room over a week and then Ged would come down with whoever from the record label, have a look and see if we couldn't sign at least one of those acts."

"I thought it was a really good idea 'cause you get that thing where scouts are constantly looking at bands and constantly bringing them in to the office, and this was like, 'No, hold on a minute, let's just focus and get on with it. Let's not dick around following what everyone else is doing, let's do something different.' Darren Dixon brought [Saracuse] and about three other acts to the table. Darren was very shrewd. Where all the other scouts were running around, suddenly Darren had an office. And it was like, 'How have you done that?!' and he'd say 'Well, it was an empty office…' And suddenly he was a part of the A&R team; he was a very, very bright guy. The first time we saw the band was in this rehearsal room, Ritz in Putney."

As for the group themselves, they were later to cheerfully admit that they didn't necessarily have the final image, or even line-up, in place for their ironically-named rehearsal room outing. "We looked like a shower of shit," said Serge, "and we had a minidisk for a drummer.[24]" Regardless of how they looked, the south Leicestershire boys intrigued the record company, as Nick Raymonde remembers.

"You couldn't help but think that it was really good. It wasn't like anything else, but it could have been. I remember Ged saying, 'This is either baggy revisited or we've got something new.' Then we pitched them a deal, offered them it a week after that."

In fact, though BMG were sufficiently impressed to put their contracts where their ears were straight away, so to speak, a counter-offer from another (major) label was, in fact, forthcoming, and for more initial cash than BMG were initially offering, but in the event (and quite rightly, too), Saracuse found that they, as individuals and as artists, were much more enamoured of Raymonde and his colleagues. The band were not purely seduced by a fatter cheque book, which is an impressive early maturity on display.

"You have to go through this painful process," continues Nick Raymonde, "where you can't say anything but equally you have to be cautious about how you do this deal. Because I have always been of the view that for this to work everything has to be right, you know, the band's gotta be really nice people, people that you want to go on holiday with; the manager's got to be a really good person; the marketing people have got to really get what your vision is, and have their own vision for it; the promo people have got to think they've got a significant chance of having a crack at it – *and everybody did*. So I think from that perspective Ged was very intuitive because he wouldn't make a knee-jerk reaction – he'd get a sense from everybody else in the record company as well about the group. So when the group was signed it wasn't a one-person signing, it was '*We've* signed Saracuse [collectively]'."

And so it transpired that after a period of missed phonecalls and uncertainty, the deal was, indeed, done to the relief of all concerned. Saracuse, Now Under New Management (specifically, the experienced Graeme Lowe of 3M Management, who was also looking after Black Rebel Motorcycle Club), signed to the record company that was already home of fellow electronic/rock/experimental fusion/music-baiters, Reading's Cooper Temple Clause. That band is quite important, too.

CHAPTER SIX

Not That Long Ago, In A Cowshed Far, Far Away...

In deepest Berkshire, an old cowshed had, since around 1998, been home to Reading's experimental rock/electronic/punk act the Cooper Temple Clause. The band were firmly entrenched as one of the more interesting acts of their era, and whilst Saracuse had been exploring and refining their own sonic palate, the Coopers had been bashing down boundaries between genres and sub-genres from the word go, hiring out not a succession of dingy rehearsal rooms, but finding instead a disused shed on a farm near their Reading home.

"Our top tip for being in a band is this," Keiran Mahon, keyboardist and bassist for the Coopers, told the author. "You've got to have your own world to live in, to socialise in and breathe in, to escape to. We were lucky that we had one just round the corner of our school in the middle of nowhere where we could make noise until four, five in the morning and never get into any trouble. And that's where all of our ideas were formulated, the ethic of us just hanging out and entertaining each other rather than any grand takeover plan of the world. It was just quite organic, just enjoying each other's company and collecting musical instruments along the way."

The Coopers built up a rabid and loyal fanbase, who would attend all of their gigs across the country, whilst concurrently and diligently collecting all the releases on the imprint that BMG had set up to release their material, Mourning Records. Although it was essentially still a BMG project – as the band were signed to that label – everything the Coopers put out was effectively therefore released, to all intents and purposes, independently, with a small and effective team in the background to make sure that things ran smoothly and remained within the ethos of the band's career. This is not necessarily the way things always work in the music industry, so not only were the Coopers trailblazers as musicians, they were also on the verge of new strategic frontiers in a more general record label sense. The cowshed was a piece of genius, not only because it afforded the band a haven away from the usual book-it-and-hope-the-PA-works-on-both-sides trek round different rehearsal spaces, its unusual location and context was also a gift for other essential parts of a band's profile-building.

"It became somewhere that you could *take* people because they made it their own place," explains Nick Raymonde. "So, if it was a journalist early doors [in a band's career], instead of me saying, 'Come and see them play at the Camden Monarch,' I'd go, 'Do yourself a favour, spend the afternoon with me, come in the car, we'll drive out to Reading – you'll love it. Even if you never write about it in your magazine, you will really enjoy this day – you'll be able to put it in your book, at least!' And people would come, and when they came they would walk away fans because they were in that room with all those boys, with all their madness and their crazy shit hanging on the wall. It was brilliant. And they'd all sit on the floor playing, superb, a drummer in the corner in a room that's ten by ten. Superb."

Raymonde, in fact, as a gentleman and a scholar also knew his rock history. "I was a huge Captain Beefheart fan," he smiles. "I loved it. I saw this film about how they made [the influential 1969 album] *Trout Mask Replica* and I could never work out how they'd managed to make a record that sounded like that at the time. I was a frustrated guitarist, a shit musician listening and wondering how they made this record, 'cause I was always interested in that. It turned out that he'd got a house in the middle of nowhere for them all, bought a bag of very, very strong lysergic acid, and they just lived in this house for about a year; they didn't have any money, they used to go out and steal chickens and food, and he wouldn't let them out of the house until the record was made, so they made it in that house. And in nineteen-whatever-it-was when they made that record, it was an extraordinary thing to have done. And that was the reason that when I saw Cooper Temple Clause in that room [it] reminded me of that situation because I thought that was a great idea, and it seemed to work so well that I thought I'd do it [again, with Saracuse]."

"I said to them, 'You need a base because Number 1, you've got to get good, and Number 2, you've got to develop a persona as a band that people are gonna buy into, irrespective of whether you do a show or not, 'cause the likelihood is when you do your first show there'll be three people and a dog there.' And that's never an easy call for someone to get excited about it, you might get the odd person who takes a flyer but generally people want to feel a bit comforted by the fact that there's more than just them and the promoter standing in the venue. We talked about it, a small budget for that to happen which was included in their advance, and they said, 'Yeah we should be able to sort that out, we know a few people', and literally two weeks later we were having pizza together and they said they'd found somewhere, it was a mate of theirs with a farm near where they all lived and he had a room available."

"I went up there about two or three weeks later and basically they had the farm. The bloke, he had a massive amount of outbuildings, he was such a huge fan of the band – he wanted to manage them, produce them, be in the band, write all the songs, sign them, everything! But he was just this really, really nice bloke and although he had all those aspirations they were completely fantasy-driven and actually the best thing that he could do for the band was to let them use his place."

Which, fantastically, he did. The farm, at Rutland Water, was to become legendary, not only for its creative atmosphere and the sense of isolated magic it fostered, but for its parties too. Writing songs means communicating emotions, after all, so the more of them you can experience, the better the songs will be. Stands to reason, doesn't it?

A farm in south Leicestershire, Omnichord in hand, however, is not the place for a band called Saracuse, something of which Chris Karloff was well aware. He'd been, as usual, busy with his head in a book. This particular one happened to be about Charles Manson, the notorious Sixties character whose 'Family' was responsible for a series of terrible acts culminating in several murders including that of Sharon Tate. Manson was himself convinced that the murders would set in motion a chain of events that would themselves lead to 'Helter Skelter', an apocalyptic final battle between races. Notwithstanding that 'Family' was already the unfortunate moniker of a Sixties band from Leicester, Karloff was also much enamoured of the surname of one of the Family, who was given immunity from prosecution due to testifying against other Family members.

Her name?

Linda Kasabian.

MOVEMENT

CHAPTER SEVEN

Farmyard Fun

The newly-monikered band may have spent half their time partying at the farm, but make no mistake, Kasabian were there to work hard, too. "[The record label] were a bit wary at first," Serge commented later as to the notion that they should also record their own debut album at the farm. "We just told them that it was going to be the best fucking debut album of all time and they should let us do it."[25] The band certainly had the space, physically and mentally, to explore any horizon that took their fancies, and although the accommodation was rather basic, with Karloff, Dibs, Serge and Meighan all bedding down in the same room, they very quickly gathered round them the accoutrements necessary for having a whole lot of fun with music.

"They weren't ready, they weren't good enough [to play live]," says Nick Raymonde of the very early days at the farm. "They didn't really have a sound, they just had a load of noises on tape that they played to, effectively. You could hear the songs but they couldn't really play it live 'cause it would have looked like a band playing to a backing track." Things soon improved, however, due to the unique closeness the band was forced into through their shared vision.

"Whereas Cooper Temple Clause lived away [from their cowshed]," continues Raymonde, "Kasabian actually lived in this place, so it made it even more intense.

So, of course, in all the things they were doing, they were beautifully *not* objective. They were completely subjective, completely myopic on what their musical proposition was. So everything they did was, 'Great' and then they'd do something else. They were never going away from it, going, 'Hmm, I'm not sure whether this is going to work,' they just kept driving on and I think that paid off enormously." Not immediately financially, of course. Despite signing up with some of the best management in the business, despite the recording contract and despite the fact that they were now on the roster of one of the UK's premier booking agents at International Talent Booking (ITB), cashflow was so severe at times that the band hardly had enough to feed or clothe themselves.

"My favourite story," laughs Ben Cole, "is when Chris Karloff's mum and dad went up to the farm to take Chris and Jim out for a meal – and Chris came out with trousers on that had no [stitching in the] seams. I think at the time it was because they were so impoverished, and they were all living in the same room in this shack even though it was massive, he was wearing these trousers with absolutely no seams on them and it was just four bits of material flapping around in the breeze! And Chris was like, 'Well, you know, I can't afford to buy any trousers.' It was a really bizarre thing."

Life and music are about getting things done whilst having fun. Although the lads had many parties, and even impromptu gigs, at Rutland Water Farm (aka Plaggy Bag Factory), it was hardly salubrious. Karen Pirie, who was working at that time for BBC Leicester, recalls: "It was like a house version of those rubbishy rehearsal rooms and studios that you see," she told the author. "Dog-eared sofas, overflowing ashtrays, piles of stuff in the corner that nobody knows who it belonged to, that kind of thing. But it was nice and just a great opportunity for them to land upon the place and be able to do that kind of thing that other bands manufacture. By living together to start with, they were really doing that, they were all mates and from relatively humble beginnings. Countesthorpe and Blaby are really unassuming parts of Leicester, they're not even from the city, just ordinary blokes who are really passionate about music.

It would be the perfect place for a house party 'cause it was so rambling, and in terms of being able to make noise, the barns and the garden and things like that were great. They did mention that they had parties and people could just crash over there – you'd have to 'cause it was so far away from everywhere that you'd have to go for the best part of the weekend. They did say they had some good parties there. It's at least twenty-five minutes from Leicester. The fact that they were in the middle of nowhere meant that they could make any noise they wanted at any time of the day so that must have given them a lot of creative freedom as well."

Even whilst the group were beginning to head out on the road during 2002 and 2003, playing all over the UK under their new moniker and picking up that elusive fanbase, when they returned to their own domain, they started to set about recording the ideas and refining the songs which were moving ever further away from their previous Saracuse blueprint. It was bringing their new record label a lot of pleasure as to the way that things were developing, with the ever sharp Nick Raymonde and his team becoming exceedingly excited about what they were beginning to hear.

"They had this one room where they basically set up all the gear," continues Raymonde, "I went down and listened to it and thought, 'This is really good, it's great'; and suddenly, because of where it was, and how they'd set it up, how strange it all was, to me it was, 'Now, this is interesting, this isn't Ged and I'm saying it could go either way, this has gone the right way. It's definitely not a reinvention of baggy, it's definitely something different'. They'd written a couple of new songs and it'd all become a little more eccentric if you like, the bleepiness of it and all the funny little noises and we hadn't said anything to them about what they should be doing musically, that just came to them as a result of being in this environment."

Ash Hannis, soon to become the band's full-time live sound engineer, was a regular visitor to the farm, and he remembers being pleased when he saw the lads' growing collection of albums.

"What was really weird," he told the author, "was the first time I stayed on the farm and realised how influenced they were by film scores and stuff. Proper full-on orchestral scores. You'd go into the games room on the farm and there was this old valve stereo there, a proper old stereo and just *so* much vinyl. It was unbelievable. Pretty much old classical music, old film scores and I think that's where they got their influences from for some of the stuff that was going on in the backing tracks. It was really interesting the first time I was up there, it was not what I expected. I probably expected your usual Oasis and Britpop-era stuff, but from hearing them I thought, 'You like Primal Scream, the Mondays, Oasis' 'cause we're the same age and that's my era. I was happy to see the fact that they had proper film scores, I was impressed. We'd listen to Classic FM on the way home in the van sometimes, it was nuts! I'd say a lot of it was Karloff, he was heavily influenced by that kind of stuff. Within the band, it's a wide and varied taste in music which is really good. I've been in quite a few bands when they've all been into the same stuff and it's like, 'Oh God', but with this lot it's all over the shop and pretty much covered every genre there was, which was wicked."

Broad musical influences or not, the group were still a member down, arguably, and with there being nobody to pound the drums at this point, Neil Ridley suggested to the band that a friend of his, the professional drummer Alex Thompson, might be a good chap to give them that solid backbeat and visual aspect that a truly exceptional sticksman can bring to a band.

"I'm from Luttleworth which is right near where they were," Thompson explained in an interview for this book. "We've a mutual friend, a friend of Tom Meighan's who we knew from school. Neil kept suggesting me for 'this band that a friend of his had signed that needed a drummer', so basically I just went along to their farmhouse near Rutland Water. I don't think at the same time they were desperate for me to join or anything. It was mainly management saying, 'Give this guy a try.'"

Which, of course, they did, as neither Alex Thompson nor Kasabian had anything to lose by hooking up for a day of chat and jamming. Thompson looks back fondly at what is loosely called an 'audition' but in reality is about so much more than the music.

"The guys all looked so different [to what you see now]," he continues. "Chris Edwards looked like a car mechanic, he had a baseball cap on and stuff – now you see them and they're so incredibly styled with their crazy haircuts and loads of stylish clothes but [back then] they properly looked like your mates from the garage or something! I remember sitting in the kitchen chatting with them for a bit but the room we went and played in was very dingy, it looked like this very scary, 'murder' kind of place.[26] I think when they played me their music we went to an upper level bedroom. It was almost student accommodation, the way the beds were out on the floor, but it looked like they'd settled in nicely. It was an impressive place to have if you could keep it but it wasn't scary apart from the room we played in, a sort of earthy floor kind of area."

Thompson's skill on the drums wasn't necessarily an advantage. Although the band were impressed with the way that he helped them to sound as they ran through two or three tracks, that was only part of what Kasabian were looking for. Any group has its own personality, a gang mentality that protects the members from the insanities and inanities of life on the road, and with Kasabian all living together in a very odd situation in an eight hundred year old farmhouse, anyone potentially joining the group would also have to have the right personality to mesh into the humour, self-belief and footy-terrace closeness that Edwards, Karloff, Meighan and Pizzorno had developed over some seven years of drinking, smoking and jamming. Thompson and the band may have sounded great together, but as people they didn't quite gel to the right extent necessary to develop that matey vibe of *us-against-the-world* further.

"We didn't really hit it off," confirms Thompson. "And if I'm honest, I didn't really feel that it was really something I wanted to do. You know that kind of thing where you don't really get on that well immediately. But it was fun, I think we only really played through something a couple of times. I think Tom was videoing it, I remember him dancing around videoing it. In hindsight, I've got friends who've roadied for them and stuff and I hear about the band from them so I [now] understand what it's all about, but we come from different places. They have that particular approach to music and I'm a more relaxed sort of person so we didn't really get on. I like to think that they didn't think too little of the drumming. We only did those two different songs but played them each a couple of times so there wasn't a lot of time spent there. Dare I say it, they already knew I could play drums 'cause I was a professional drummer but it was more about getting to know each other and trying it out." So they tried, but it didn't work. Nothing gained, but nothing lost either.

So no harm done: Alex Thompson cheerfully toddled off to hit things extremely skilfully behind a young man with an interesting taste in woolly hats and beards from Manchester, one Damon Gough, who is perhaps better known as Badly Drawn Boy. As for Kasabian, the realisation that they needed to find someone who understood the peculiar dynamic of their activities was growing stronger, and they were to turn briefly to one of their old mates, the gifted DJ Daniel Ralph Martin, who was beginning to learn how to play drums too.

"I wasn't offended that they wanted to get their mate in 'cause anyone would, wouldn't they?" posits Thompson in conclusion. "If you've got a choice between getting your mate in or some professional drummer that you don't really know, who you just know through someone else? I didn't take it personally at the time, I wasn't really giving off vibes of, 'My God! This is what I was born to do!' either. But I have no idea of what songs we did. I definitely remember Tom jumping around with a video camera to his face so there is video evidence of [the audition] unless he's taped over it with *Neighbours* or something!"

"Everyone was asking who I was gonna get to produce the record," recalls Raymonde, "and I didn't have a clue," he cheerfully admits. "You've either got to get someone who snapshots it, just records it [as it sounds in the rehearsal space live] and gets a lucky break, 'cause they could play the same song three times and it would sound completely different at that point. So I said to them, 'Why don't you actually try to record it here?' They looked at me like I was *fucking mad*. I said, 'All you've gotta do is get a bit of gear that you can record this on,' and one of them said, 'Yeah, we can use the room upstairs' and the bloke on the farm said they could use the room; now they had a studio, a recording place downstairs, their sleeping bags above it and another room off it where they were recording it all down to a cheap hard drive set-up.

Two weeks later, I went down there and nearly choked 'cause it was really close [to sounding perfect]. It wasn't *quite* there because obviously they didn't have the ability to mix it properly; they were just recording it. Also, Serge, who was really the producer in a sense in the band, was also discovering at the time how it could all be put together – he was doing a really good job and he was surprising himself. And that was when we decided that we needed to get a producer in but he would need to be someone who could basically stay there with them and that wasn't going to be easy."

Indeed it was not. A producer not only needs to understand the band's music, but also their different personalities. He needs to be referee, goalkeeper, assistant manager and hardworking midfielder rolled into one, and in the case of this unique band who lived on a farm in the middle of nowhere, the producer would also have to have a lot of time for ideas from out of the left-field too.

CHAPTER EIGHT

New Jack City

In an intriguing twist in the Kasabian tale, the guy that stepped forward for this unusual task wasn't even really what you could even term a producer, at least not in the conventional sense. Maverick? Certainly. Musical? Near-genius. Remixer? None better. Producer? Inexperienced, at best. His name was, and probably still is, Garret 'Jacknife' Lee, and he came to the attention of BMG on the back of some superb mash-ups he'd been making.

"Darren Dixon introduced me to this guy, Jacknife Lee, who'd been making bootlegs," says Raymonde. "*Really* good ones. He was young and he'd made some recordings that I heard and thought the band would like, I played it to them and they really liked the stuff. I told them I didn't know if he could do it or not, but that I would meet him. I met him and he was such an interesting bloke; he was just fascinating and he'd listened to the demos that Serge had just done in this room. And he started to put it into a context which I admit I didn't really understand to start with because he started to give it film references and stuff.

He was talking about Sergio Leone and Ennio Morricone, and he was referencing all these things, but then started talking about all the films of that genre, film noir and art-house films that reference all those sorts of things. He was very eloquent and I thought he'd also be able to connect not just on a musical level with the band but actually on an intellectual level. I could say that 'intellectual' is the wrong word but that band are intellectual. They're really clever. Tom, for all his sword-fighting, musketeerish bravado, that bloke is a very deep thinker. He has to be to come up with all this stuff. Serge is a very deep thinker as well. As they all are. I could sit down with them for hours and talk about all sorts of things that were nothing to do with music and so could Jacknife Lee so I got him to meet them."

Instant sparks.

"Nick Raymonde called me in for a meeting, and played me demos including 'Processed Beats'," Jacknife recounted exclusively for this book. "I loved it. I had never produced a proper record before, just bits and pieces. My remixes were making waves, and I had a hit of sorts with my Missy Elliot and Eminem bootlegs. Nick called and asked me to do it; the band liked a Krautrock-ish song I did for the movie *28 Days Later*. We met at the farm and liked each other."

Great as the initial meeting may have been, Jacknife wasn't a huge fan of the Rutland Water set-up in the comfort stakes as sessions for the album began to take place. "It was fucking freezing, that farm!" he says. "I don't think I slept on a bed, maybe I did, or it may have been a couch. [But] they all slept in one room. PlayStation, smokes, porn and Alan Partridge! The farm was crucial for them becoming a gang, a proper band. It was isolated, and all they thought about was music. Tom is very intense and with the cabin fever of the farm the whole thing was a bit mental: young men, isolated, nothing to do but music, smoke, drink ... things do get odd. In a very good way though. All bands should begin like this."

Jacknife and the band began to try to mould the various bits and pieces with which the band had been doodling into pictures of a more panoramic nature. No mean feat: whilst in the Saracuse days, the focus was firmly on *songs*, in the confines of the farm, with all its attendant indulgences and musical explorations, the focus was on *noises*, on *sounds*. This is what would go towards making an exceptional final result, but the path to get there was muddy and fraught with problems. The band had already been busy on at least making sure that the tracks they were to record were conceptually ready.

"The [songs] were mapped out," continues Jacknife. "Great ideas, but recorded on cheap equipment. It was all there though, lyrics done, melodies were there. Serge is brilliant. He had it all pretty much worked out on his PC – he has a great mind. At the time they were listening to a lot of Warp Records artists, and prog rock, so it was very electronic and this is the way we started, coming at it from a more programmed angle. I would [then] take the [audio] files and sort them out. We discussed what live instruments would be put on there, and away we'd go."

One live instrument that wasn't going well, however, was the situation with the drummer, who, as he was still finding his way round the kit, wasn't up to the standard required, technically, by the band at the time.

"The first session," continues Jacknife, "was pretty bad in terms of drumming… [he was] a friend of theirs, but he couldn't actually *play* [to the standard required] so straight away I suggested we get someone else."

"If you're a serious band," offers Alex Thompson, "you can't have that kind of thing. I think they wanted to be punk rock and have their mate in the band but it didn't work out and somewhere someone was saying, 'Listen lads, you need to get a proper drummer in.'"

The answer was closer to the Kasabian project than anyone might have thought at first. Enter Portsmouth-based Mitch Glover, raconteur, gentleman and, wearing another hat, drummer with the band Kosheen, also signed to BMG. Glover was also, when not on tour, bringing in the pennies, as many musicians do, by teaching his instrument to those just starting to play.

"I was teaching Dan, their original [guy] who wanted to be their drummer," Mitch recalled when I interviewed him for this book. "He was like a mate of theirs. The label wanted me to teach Dan to get him up to scratch to join the band, 'cause he was sort of the weaker member, playing-wise. Dan did one session with me and the label wanted me to get back to them and let them know how it was going on. It was a bit of a distance [for him] to travel from Leicester to Portsmouth … so the label were like asking me, 'Right, okay, can you step in?' sort of thing."

Neil Ridley, whose belief in Kasabian was shatterproof, was still keen on passing the job on to his good friend Alex Thompson, who was resolute that it was not for him. "I remember Neil saying to me, 'Are you sure you don't want to go for it 'cause this guy [Mitch Glover] is really up for it,'" laughs Thompson. "And I said, 'Not really, no.' I don't regret it at all, I don't know if I sound like I do 'cause it's still not my kind of music really and not the kind of thing that I like to do. Obviously there's other things about it but I think you've got to enjoy what you do. I think you've got to enjoy what you're playing when you're doing music otherwise it can look quite fake."

Eloquently put. Mitch Glover, was, indeed 'really up for it', and had already analysed the style of his pupil, Daniel Ralph Martin. "Dan was basically a beginner drummer," he says. "So in the sense of what he was doing to the tracks it was really straight down the path, no dynamics, no building with certain parts of the track. When he played, it was in a really jazz sort of style, timid and by then I'd been on the road for about six years so I was *hammering* the drums. I don't think the guys had worked with many drummers before that, so it was kind of a refreshing tint put to their tunes. Dynamically I came in and built with the tunes, certain sections you played more chilled out and then built with it whereas before I think Dan just *played* it [straight]. Cause that's all he could do. Bless him, 'cause he's a nice bloke, but he couldn't nail it properly. I was chatting to Serge and he was saying it was nice to have someone who could fill out all the gaps. Cause there's a lot of gaps [musically][27] and I think at the time as well, Serge and the two Chrisses were sort of still learning and I had a lot more experience. So I was going for a big drum sound, visually and playing-wise and it was kind of helping them along." To be fair to Dan, it was a big ask to get up to professional recording standards so quickly, so none of these comments should be read as criticism; besides, on the decks he's a damned wizard.

With Mitch in the hot-seat, it was time to head out and do some serious gigging around the country. The first 'proper' gig Kasabian did with Mitch Glover drumming was in Wrexham's Central Station venue in January 2003, and the sticksman recorded it for posterity.

"The guys didn't want to record anything at the time," he says. "I was like, 'Well, you might as well, 'cause then you can hear yourselves back.' Everyone was kind of learning their trade at the time, they were quite young lads and I had a few years on them, but nothing major. But they were a little bit cautious on what to record and what not to record. Prior to that gig there was a bucketload of rehearsals for about a month and a half."

The label themselves were getting rather excited about the group by this point, having heard the initial Rutland Water Farm[28] demos developing in conjunction with Jacknife Lee, who was alternating between spending time with the band down at the farm and arranging additional recording sessions at various venues.[29]

With the help of Mitch on board, the band's live work was beginning to storm and wow audiences throughout the UK, the Kasabian sound appeared to be coalescing neatly, with the label, the producer and the band all pulling in the same direction. A commanding triumvirate indeed, but despite the initial excitement about the album's genesis, there was a schism beginning to appear between the group's vision and that of the producer, and it was to prove ultimately insurmountable.

"They were a gang," recalls Jacknife Lee. "All chipped in ideas and [it was] very democratic. They came to London; I think we did 'Reason Is Treason' first and it turned out wonderfully." Democratic it might have been, but on occasion the studio sessions would engender a rather odd atmosphere, particularly considering some of the pronouncements of the ever-ebullient Meighan.

Lee is better qualified than most to explain the creative dynamic within the nascent band, "[Tom's] brilliant and comes at things from such a strange angle. I didn't know if he was a genius or ...

Chris [Karloff] and Serge battled a little. Chris was always cautious, nervous ... The band were very enthusiastic and warm; Tom and Serge cried when we recorded strings on one song. They were sweet and earnest. Unafraid of their emotions."

Sadly, however, the relationship between the talented Jacknife Lee and the exploration-loving group was fragmenting fast. One of the main jobs of any producer is to ensure that, no matter what, the sessions are not only productive but also, as much as possible, enjoyable. Conversely, in the particular case of Kasabian, the band were also being encouraged by their record label to follow their noses in a sonic sense more than probably any other band preparing to launch themselves out into the music biz on debut. To put it simply, more song-based groups would have found laying down the tracks a breeze. It is often the case that by the time a band reaches the stage of recording their debut album, they have been performing, refining and tweaking those ten to twelve tracks for years in the live arena, throwing out the dodgy ones and getting the best ones to a high standard of user-friendliness and confidence before laying the definitive versions down to tape. The album, therefore, is quite often a very quick process that requires what Nick Raymonde would call more of a 'snapshot' approach on the part of the producer: that is to say, more or less capturing the sound and the energy of the live set that has been wowing crowds and basically the sound that had led to the band in question having been identified as signings by their label in the first instance.

Of course, in the case of the Blaby bunch, their live set had been considerably different in the Saracuse days, and by the time it came down to getting the 'definitive' Kasabian sound down into a recorded form, they'd distanced themselves from their early incarnation and as a result there were not the same kind of solid, played-a-hundred-times tracks from which to work. Garret Lee had been brought in precisely because he had been identified as a fellow soul with the musical and creative empathy to facilitate the moulding, or translating, of the band's newish and more experimental ethos into a reasonably palatable musical area, which necessitated a very deep connection with the band themselves. That would often mean pulling songs apart and rebuilding them from their constituent beats and loops, and just as often standing back and refining what was already there. Perhaps because of the essentially fluid creative process, however, his role was rather closer to that of an auxiliary band member than that for which the group themselves were ultimately prepared, according to Chris Edwards at least.

"We wanted to record it ourselves and take it to a mixer but the record label recommended we work with [Lee]," he recalled. "It just wasn't working. He was basically ripping the songs apart and trying to redo them. They weren't dirty enough. We did 'Reason Is Treason' and he totally got what we were doing because he came to the farm for a few days and he knew what we were on about."[30] The band was far less enamoured of the studio sessions that Lee and the group set up in London, finding them overly clean-sounding when a little less polish and a little more punk rock was closer to the group's hearts.

"They had never been to a studio before (sic)," continues Jacknife. "So we were really starting from scratch; they had no experience whatsoever. They did need guidance, but my guidance was slightly off from where they wanted to go, which is why the sessions broke down. I was [just] trying to get the record finished. We did eight songs, but it changed towards the end when problems arose between the label, the band and me."

One thing that would have had a huge impact on matters was Nick Raymonde moving on from BMG, in March 2003. The charismatic Raymonde had been the guy responsible for instigating the initially extremely fruitful relationship between Lee and Kasabian, and with his considerable personality removed from the situation, the creative forces of the producer and his charges began to clash, and it finally came to a head over the track, 'Rain', which had appeared both on the Bink Bonk demos and also in various permutations down the years in the Saracuse and Bedrock days. It was epic, for sure, but a firmly *indie*-epic track and rather tied to the Oasis/Stereophonics-led tunes that the group were leaving behind at a rate of knots. Nonetheless, because it was such a damned good track, there was pressure there for Kasabian to get it down on tape.

"A good song," muses Jacknife Lee. "But not right for the way the band sounded. I think we attempted it, but never finished it. Things were getting very odd. The band would come to the studio and not want to play anything." Momentum was stalling. Eventually, the relationship was terminated and Jacknife Lee went off to work with, among others, Snow Patrol.[31]

What Kasabian had to their advantage, of course, was the farm set-up, and between bouts of live work, it was to there they returned. Serge's growing wizardry on the equipment and the band's determination to get things right without outside input meant that they were uniquely in a position to discuss the way to proceed next.

"We wanted it to be more organic," explained Edwards, "[But Jacknife Lee] ended up kind of changing our music a bit too much … it just wasn't working. So we just told the label to let us produce it ourselves, and then we'll get some guy to mix it."[32]

A typical understatement.

CHAPTER NINE

Into The Abbiss

Enter Jim Abbiss, rising star of production and the man responsible for the sonics on several of Kasabian's favourite albums of the era, including those of DJ Shadow and spiritual dance-rock groovemates The Music. Abbiss' familiarity with the dance and indie scenes made him the perfect choice to come in and add his experience to the songs that were being moulded at the farm.

"I got a call from the label saying that they had a couple of tracks they wanted finishing off and mixing, which the band had done a lot of work on," Abbiss explained in an interview for this book. "[Kasabian had] quite a disparate selection of tunes, some of which were half-finished, some done by one person, some collaborations, whatever, different producers and mixers, and they just wanted to see if I was into the stuff and would I mix a tune?"

Fortunately, Jim Abbiss was well into it, and the production situation was settled once more. Initially he mixed an album track to be called 'Club Foot', and the results pleased the band immensely. "It was one of those few magical moments in your career when you do something and instantly feel a kinda rapport with people, 'cause they just came down and wanted to hear it twenty times in a row 'cause they loved it, and it just felt really good. So we kinda got together and I got sent a lot more tunes and we went through them and worked out what we'd do with them."

As it transpired, the band kept the audio takes flowing toward Jim Abbiss, and he found a definite pattern developing with what he heard, in terms of vibe as much as anything else.

"I got sent [various] versions of tunes [in progress]," he explains. "I went through them and said, 'I like this version of this tune and this version of this tune, and that one sounds done' and I ended up picking pretty much, on every occasion, what they'd recorded at the farm. And it seemed to me that the beauty of the farm was that it gave them endless sort of time to mess about with stuff and try new ideas out.

My work mainly is production, I do a lot less mixing these days, so I normally start projects from scratch, but you never know when you're going to enter into a project and that one I entered it fairly late on. I just don't think they were completely happy with where they were I guess. There may've been a couple of [different] versions of tunes and they've taken bits from them so you'd have this tune that was kinda going along doing its thing, and then something just completely bonkers would come in, because it maybe came from another version or [whatever]. Who knows, I don't know how they arrived at it, but there were some properly trippy moments in it and it seemed as though when they did things more formally in the studio in that first album, a lot of that stuff was kinda ironed out and then re-injected by someone afterwards, and I personally don't think that's ever a very interesting way of doing it. I mean, if I'm doing a band from scratch, the hardest things to do are to inject craziness into it."

Precisely: one of the main reasons for renting the farm in the first place was to allow the music to grow organically and independently of any outside context. The sticking point had come, of course, when the more restrictive studio-type requirements came into play.

"It's either got *it* or it hasn't," continues the producer. "You can't sit down and do some mad effects [afterwards], 'cause it all sounds contrived and nonsense to me. And those things normally happen through mistakes or through the band messing around with things themselves; by their own admission [they] didn't know much about recording but they knew enough of things they liked … there's loads of organic sounds on it, and it's a kind of mixture really. One of the reasons I love [the debut Kasabian album] is because it's a great mixture of electronica and organic stuff, and I think it does it very well."

With the recordings being given the final sheen by Abbiss (and his engineer, Simon 'Barny' Barnicott), it was time for Kasabian to ramp it up some more in the live arena, embarking again on audience-grabbing appearances around the country, now with live sound wizard Ash 'Acky' Hanning twiddling the knobs and making the increasingly complex sounds make sense.

"I'd done them a couple of times in Coventry, and a couple of times in Sumo," Ash muses. "It was their first big, 'proper' gig in Sumo when there was like a proper sell-out show, two hundred and eighty punters or something downstairs – it was fucking rammed. Graeme Lowe happened to be there and said, 'Right, I like the way you mix, you're on board' and that was it – Bang! Off I went for three and a half years on the road!

Touring is such a fucking ball. Such a laugh. You're skint, basically, if you're on the road, but you have such a laugh. If you've a month on tour it's a month-long party. Obviously you've got a job to do, and you've got to be on for that but basically you do a bit of a gig, have a bit of a party, crash out, wake up, go to a new gig, have a bit of a party, crash out, wake up, go to a new gig, have a bit of a party, crash out, wake up, go to a new gig, and then have a day off and that fucks you! The second you get a day off, your body shuts down and you think, 'Oh God, not a day of rest,' 'cause you're knackered.

We didn't have solid tours but when they were off, they were off for quite a while. I was doing another band and a club night as well, so I was pretty much seven days a week solid. So if they were in Sheffield doing a show, I'd leave them that night, come back to Coventry on the train, do a show here 'cause they were on a travel day to Glasgow or something that day, then I'd literally hop on a flight from Coventry to Glasgow and nine times out of ten beat them to the gig! It used to make me laugh 'cause they were on an eight hour drive and I was like, a forty minute flight and there we go! You can't beat touring, it's so much fun out on the road but it is bloody hard work. You have to be switched on, it doesn't matter what you were doing the night before or what else is going on, you've got to be switched on for that show."

All the elements were beginning to come together, including a rather interesting logo which first found its way into the beginnings of popular view on a demo circulated to select journalists, including Ian Abraham, who at the time was editor of 'Ones To Watch', an influential section of new bands bible *The Fly Magazine* that concentrated on the very fastest, rising young potential superstars.

"I'd heard the name," he told me. "Foolishly, when I heard that a band had signed to a major back then and I knew they were going to have money chucked at them then it was within my interest to check them out to see whether or not they were going to go [on to bigger things]."

He recalls receiving said demo CD with the name of the band misspelt, as 'Kasabien'. The tracks on it are the Bink Bonk version of 'Processed Beats' plus the ultimately troublesome 'Rain In My Soul' and the remix of 'Gone So Far', both of which were taken from the Bedrock sessions. The artwork also had a crude, hand-drawn character for the CD's on-body print: a man, looking something like a guerrilla freedom fighter, with what looked like a handkerchief obscuring half of his face.

"The demo had not a thing written on it and I didn't know anything about it other than it was sent to me, to the Barfly and another A&R scout that I know. I didn't know how many, it was all printed and 'Kasabien' (sic) was printed in the same font as the real spelling was on the mailout. And the track names were written in the same font. Apparently Saracuse sent me a demo too but I think I threw it away 'cause it was fucking pony."

What all this does illustrate is that even as the group's live appearances were beginning to 'cause some real rumblings in certain quarters, the fact that demos including what might still be reasonably shown as late Saracuse-era material were still circulating is testament to the continuing exploration going on behind the scenes and the continuing surgery that was needed to mould the extant audio into a comprehensible album sound. The logo itself was part of the ongoing campaign to come up with musically and visually arresting concepts to introduce the group to the world.

"There's no point just having a name," explained Tom. "It's something to look at." The intent being that the Kasabian Man would serve as a powerful statement of what the band were all about on its own merits.

"The guy behind the mask on our sleeves and our posters isn't Che Guevara or Chairman Mao," continued Meighan, chatting to Ian Abraham. "He's just the bloke on the bus, living his own little revolution. That's kind of what we're doing. We've got 'the menace' as well, you know. He just represents us as people. We see him and know there's something going on."

This would become increasingly important as time went by, with Kasabian's fans becoming set to mobilise themselves into something a little more formalised than merely coming to the gigs and making a hell of a racket. In the meantime, however, there was a small logistical problem beginning to rear its head, with drummer Mitch Glover finding that his commitments with Kosheen were beginning to clash with his Kasabian gigs.

"To be honest with you, Kosheen were on a back-to-back major UK tours and a priority for the record label," he explains. "And at the time Kasabian were playing proper out of the way pubs in the middle of a field or something, to get experience and to get the guys up to scratch with their playing and stuff. The boys wanted me to join, but they knew I was in Kosheen and they were quite respectful of that. It was really, really awkward … you can't just walk out of one and go into the other! I really enjoyed doing both but I'd done that solidly for a year and it sort of ended up running myself right into a brick wall, workwise. I knew it was gonna happen, but the timing was so awkward. I think if Kosheen weren't recording or majorly touring, if it was quiet for the band I could have got someone else in to replace me, and I could have made the move. But it was just too awkward with the way things were working out. At the time it was the right decision."

In retrospect, there was no decision to be made, and although Kasabian were beginning to gain attention in the press and the odd bit of radio play, Kosheen were way advanced of their Leicester counterparts in terms of actual sales success and track record. As luck would have it, however, there was a ready-made solution in place for that troublesome drum spot – Mitchell Glover's younger brother, Ryan.

"I'd got to the point where I had to make the switch," explains Mitch, "and the label phoned me up and said, 'We know you've got a brother [who plays drums].' Cause I'd mentioned to the guys that I had a brother who was learning drums and they said, 'Great! If he's as quarter as good as you, Mitch, we've gotta have him on the kit.' They were auditioning, and Christ knows how many people were going for that job. I taught Ryan everything, I teach the drums so I coached him track by track, wrote out the parts and spent a fair bit of time with him and then he went for this audition up at the farm."

An audition at the farm, as we saw in the case of Alex Thompson, was a lot more than just being able to play the tracks nattily and hold down a backbeat, although Portsmouth-based Ryan Glover, in common with his brother, was incredibly good at doing just that.

"I went up there in August 2003," explained Ryan when I asked him. "I went all the way up to Leicester, spent all day with the guys and played some tracks that I'd been learning. The audition was at the big farmhouse in Leicester. As you walked into the house you turned left and it was what looked like some weird old stable barn type of place, but obviously they'd converted it into their rehearsal space where they did all their practicing. There was a drum kit set up there and stuff and that's where I auditioned and went over the two or three songs I'd learned that Mitch had given me. One was 'I.D.', and the one I definitely did play was 'Processed Beats'. I may have played a couple more but I don't remember because I wasn't actually *playing* that much. We did talk quite a lot and have a good old chat as well as a few jams and stuff. They knew me through Mitch and obviously they knew what Mitch was like and as a character me and my brother are quite the same. I was ready to go, I had the fire in my belly and I was ready to take on the world. I think they recognised that as well, they knew that I wasn't messing them about. If they were gonna say yes to me then they knew they'd have me fully committed which is obviously what happened. I heard about a week later, after they'd auditioned about fifteen or so other drummers in London, that they wanted me in the band.

I had to quit college, I had to quit my old band, I had to quit my job and I was up in London within two weeks rehearsing for up-and-coming gigs. It was full-on for about three weeks rehearsing, meeting management, the record label and various people behind the scenes, and we spent week after week in London until the first gig came along."

Ryan's first appearance with Kasabian was in Swansea's Patti Pavilion, supporting the Detroit band Electric Six, who had exploded into the charts with their ultra-ironic, high camp singles, 'Danger! High Voltage!' and a cover of Franz Schubert's 1818 requiem, 'Gay Bar'. Dick Valentine and his boys were riding high, which suited them very well.

"London to Swansea is a fucking long way, basically, and we had to stop at Bristol on the way back," the drummer explains. "I managed to drive down there with the bass player – it wasn't short notice, we had a few days to prepare and get things ready. I can't remember the actual reaction of the crowd, 'cause when I used to go onstage I [wore] earphones 'cause I used to play to a click track. So I never used to actually hear what the crowd was chanting, or whether they were actually interested or not! The other problem I had as well was obviously I wear glasses and I'm short-sighted so I couldn't actually see much either! That's the problem. I couldn't actually say whether the crowd loved it or not but all I can say is that after the gig, the bands were walking round the crowd checking the other bands, there was another band supporting above us, and apparently they were getting really good feedback with people walking up to them saying, 'That was a really shit hot set.'"

November 2003 was to prove something of a pivotal time in the live arena for the band, as they set out on a ten date tour of the UK as support to label mates and fellow farm-lovers, Cooper Temple Clause.

CHAPTER TEN

La Mossa

November 10, 2003 was also the official/unofficial release of 'Processed Beats', which was variously delivered to journalists as a one-sided white label vinyl promo or a simple CD encased in two pieces of cardboard which were held together by a simple elastic band. Although not a chart-aimed piece of plastic, the vinyl version was on the unusual 10" format, and came wrapped in a Kasabian flag. If it weren't already ultra-collectable, the fact that there were a mere 1,000 of those babies out there was the frosted coating on the cherry on the icing on the cake for fans and media alike. Here, indeed, was an intriguing band at last: something of an antidote to the anodyne mulch that surrounded it. Imprinted on the B-side of the vinyl, too, was the phrase 'tutti a la mossa' — Italian for 'all to the movement'. This, coupled with the Kasabian Man (a.k.a. 'Stealth') and the general approach, all began to point to something of a mysterious, almost underground phenomenon that appeared to come directly from the streets. And in a sense it was: La Mossa, The Movement, was a vital part in getting the name, artistic ethos and music of Kasabian known across the UK almost by osmosis. It was also a refinement of an American approach to band promotion known over there as Street Teaming. Kasabian's most ardent fans were invited to become part of the process itself, as original Movement member Amanda McGowan explains.

"I'd been recruited by Dan Ayers at Sony BMG who was basically running the new media section at the time, setting up a website and a forum for Kasabian," she explained in an interview for this book. "So I went down to their Cooper Temple Clause support at

Shepherd's Bush Empire and kind of helped out with collecting names and letting people know about them and that kind of thing. I was blown away by them, it was the first time that I saw them. It was wicked."

By this stage, Kasabian had seen a version of 'Processed Beats' cover mounted as a CD on the front of the *New Musical Express*, although somewhere down the line there had been something of a breakdown in communication. "They put the wrong version on it," laughs live soundman, Ash Hannis. "I remember having a fight in the van 'cause someone had stuck the wrong version on the cover, an old demo version went on instead of the proper one. A lot of the backing stuff was done on the farm then sent to Jim Abbiss' place as individual files to be remastered and remixed. There were all sorts of effects and pedals that kept breaking down all the time. I think at one point we had electroharmonics, actually bringing in synths as well, not just playing guitar. The amount of pedals we went through was ridiculous."

With the band ripping it up onstage, their fervent fans were busy beavering away to ensure that potential supporters and interested observers alike were able to find their way to the concerts. "You'd have subliminal things going on," confirms Hannis. "I've seen a lot of shows and a lot of different ways of advertising bands and this was great. They had AA signs, with the Kasabian man on it, and arrows pointing towards the venue. So you'd be walking down the street and you'd see what looked like the AA sign with the Kasabian man on it and they were everywhere. Plastered on the London Underground was what looked like an Underground sticker – but you looked at it and it was Kasabian gig dates! It was really cleverly marketed. They'd have street teams out a week before they played, whacking these things up in town directing you toward the gig so you could literally walk off the train and find out exactly where it was. They were plastered everywhere but you couldn't tell unless you were actually looking for them. You couldn't tell they were there. It was very subliminal and very clever."

And a lot of fun for those charged with informing the world about The New Band Who Were Gonna Change Music, too. There's an immense pride in being involved with launching a group from Day One onto a wider plane, and to be part of that is just as satisfying whether you're Director of A&R, the sound engineer, or one of the cheeky chaps and chapesses rushing around the UK whapping stickers up.

"It was basically a group of about twenty people who really, really liked the band and who went out and really bigged them up," continues McGowan. "We were given tools, which involved stencils and stickers ... so people would be like, 'What, who's this, what's going on?' The people who set up The Movement, the first twenty or so people, were quite scary in themselves – and I am including myself in that, I was a bit of a nutcase when I was younger! You'd stick things up wherever you wanted to put it! It originally started in the States, the street marketing thing, and people over here kind of took it and twisted it. Kasabian also had that kind of, I'm loathe to say it, but almost a Pub Rock value where they connected with people a lot onstage. Just from being disaffected youth and stuff like that."

Disaffected or not, the latter days of 2003 and the early days of 2004 were exciting ones for the early coolistas who'd got on board with Kasabian, and there was a palpable sense that here was, in fact, not just another good group a la Cooper Temple Clause who were producing exciting music, or having a wicked time onstage like The Music, but a band who could do both those things as well as having an unprecedented impact on the music scene and change it massively.

James Milton-Thompson was another very early member of The Movement, and he recalls the atmosphere of sheer excitement that had begun to engulf all associated with the Kasabian camp.

"We went to all the gigs, did all the merchandise and that. Persuading people to sign up [to the mailing list], buy the T-shirts and all that. They gave out stickers and signs to put up and you'd put them everywhere toward the venue they were playing, and give out promo things on the door. The Movement was like a revolution, revitalising British music, basically, and that's what it felt like. It was mad. The conversations we had with Tom Meighan ... we were at a gig in Birmingham in The Vale, this tiny little roof of this pub and he just said he felt like it was like another Sex Pistols or something. He was that confident. He just said, 'What a night, our band ...' just the whole buzz, it was amazing. We were sort of like their troops, following them about. They could count on their regulars like me and my mates [being there at the gigs]. This is late 2003, early 2004 when they were doing all the small venues and supporting little unsigned bands at Reading Fez Club and stuff like that."

"There were always a few people who weren't sure," reveals Amanda McGowan, "as there always are when you do something like that: 'What are you using these names for? What's this for? Are you gonna send me loads of spam?' and you're like, 'No, you're gonna become part of The Movement' and they'd say, 'Well, what is The Movement?' and you're like, 'You won't find out unless you sign up!' It's very much like a secret society ... it was a very, very exciting time and everyone could feel it. There was definitely a sense that this was going to happen. Kasabian have always had that belief, Tom in particular ... he kind of drove the band along."

Of course, you can have all the Movement members in the world scurrying about putting up signs and stencilling your logo all over the place, but it's not going to make any odds whatever to your career if you can't deliver musically. The Cooper Temple Clause tour was an acid test for a band that was still, in a sense, finding its feet, with 2003 certainly having been a year in which Kasabian learnt how to smash it up even better in the live arena. There was also one particularly strong influence on the growing musical movement that both the bands on tour together shared.

"They've definitely got that collective dance/rock crossover that people are dying for," muses Kieron Mahon of the Coopers. "That's what Primal Scream really started in the early Nineties, and every band that's done something sort of similar to them have Primal Scream to thank because they were the real innovators of that combined sound. And so were we, we were very, very indebted to what they were doing on albums like *Vanishing Point* and *XTRMNTR*."

"When we heard *XTRMNTR*, that kind of woke us up," agreed Tom Meighan. "Jesus, that's a great album. 'Kill All Hippies', when I heard that song, that changed our opinions on rock 'n' roll forever. They should be more put out there for that, Primal Scream. Big time. I really do believe that. And that's kind of kicked us off in this kind of way."

"They were *absolutely key* records for our generation to grow up with," continues Mahon. "Records that showed that you could combine different sounds. It didn't have to be just a distorted guitar and a Britpop chorus, it could be a whole load of dangerous, war-like sounds, ideally, that would be much more explosive and volatile. The kids do like that, they want to feel like they're in danger, I guess, and the more scared you can make them feel, the better! I think we always looked out to scare ourselves in the studio, and if you scare yourselves you're probably going to scare others. And if you're a six-piece dancing around onstage and bumping into the audience ..."

In many ways, the Coopers had opened a lot of doors for their labelmates, be it the fact that they shared a little of the same musical cues, or that the Coopers' own farmhouse rehearsal studios and collectable merchandise and demo/record releases were, in a real sense, something of a test-the-water blueprint for the subsequent approach that the record company took when Kasabian began to become a force to be reckoned with.

"When they were being talked about at the record label, we noticed a lot of comparisons and similarities between us," Mahon notes. "And that was good, I'm sure we weren't the only group of guys doing what we did and I'm sure we shared some of the same beliefs. It was good to have them on tour, although to be honest socially we didn't interact that much and it was a shame. It wasn't a specific plan and sometimes these things don't work out, and you keep on missing each other for any reason; life's really a constant state of flux and you can't always organise everything perfectly. But it was good to have them out on the road and they certainly helped put us forward as developing an interesting bill. We always had bands we didn't have any qualms taking out [with us] so it was good."

Which is hugely to the credit of the Cooper Temple Clause, one of the most inventive and sonically excellent groups that the UK has ever produced, and who at the time could have been forgiven for being a little more churlish or suspicious about their Leicester counterparts. However, their embracing of them to the extent of taking them out on tour was of great benefit, particularly when you consider the relative trajectories the two bands' careers were subsequently to take.

"They didn't sound like anything else [and neither did] Cooper Temple Clause," declares Nick Raymonde. "I've never really thought there was much point signing something that sounded like something else. And the fact that one had the support internally already, not only from the key elements in the company which are effectively promotion, marketing and press, but also from the President who was as fundamental in signing the group as either Darren or myself, because he was there. You were onto a winner, and here was a group that actually had pop songs and weren't scared of it. They had pop songs. So having got all of the signing done and properly set up, that's very important. Cause if you sign a group in the right environment you're onto a winner straight away. You can start spending money, or more, putting your ideas into action immediately. You don't have to wait and go, 'I wonder, could I…?' or

'Would it be okay if I…?' 'cause you know everybody's just going to say, 'Yes, of course – we've already decided we're all going to go for it so just get on with it.' So that was very important and Coopers set the way for that. Also, by then, there was this group of people who really loved the genre, but who had been used to BMG not being particularly friendly toward it, [and were] suddenly finding the doors were open and you were allowed to spend some decent money marketing these groups."

And although Nick Raymonde himself had moved onto other projects by the tail end of 2003, the belief of the record label was such that Kasabian were certainly still being availed of all the infrastructure that they needed. This was a band, an idea and a project that warranted a lot of attention from the label, which may seem to be a little of an odd thing to say, but occasionally in the music industry the loss of a key man in a particular musical project means that the best laid plans of mice[33] often come to naught.

"The support they got from the record company was superb," acknowledges Ash Hannis. "I've been working with bands on small independent labels up to full scale majors, and I've seen how badly bands can get treated, but with Kasabian they had some serious clout behind them. Straight to ITB, the top booking agents in the country; you could tell from day one that they were going to be big. I remember the Manchester show with the Coopers, where there were more people there to see Kasabian than the Coopers [who were headlining]. When Kasabian came offstage, half the room disappeared and it was like, 'Fucking hell' and that's when you think they are going to explode. It was obvious."

From a band perspective, they were working their collective balls off to put themselves across in the right way, but as Ryan Glover explains, it was more than worthwhile. "We were getting such a massive response from those gigs," he says. "A couple of times we felt a little bit hard done by 'cause we were going onstage at quarter past seven, half seven and it was like, 'Christ, is it worth it? There's only about ten people here,' but more often than not it was genuinely pretty good and by the time we'd finished there were a good few hundred people there and we were getting such a good response after [each] gig. It was a case of go on stage, kick arse and leave people wanting more. We knew we had the songs, it was just a case of how we delivered them. We went on stage, giving it that Oasis-style and fucking off, you know, giving it the attitude but being really professional at the same time. We had to go 'Bang!' and we all knew we had to go onstage and play like it was our last ever gig, because we knew, we all agreed even before the tour, that that tour was gonna be the tour that was gonna make or break us. Cause if we'd had a crap tour, who was to say that we would have got all the other gigs afterwards? So every gig we had on that tour we really enjoyed it and made the most of it onstage and just really went for it. I was really getting into my stride as far as the drums were concerned and just hitting them really hard. The fondest memory was the Portsmouth gig 'cause obviously that was my hometown one and all my friends and family were there. It was pretty nerve-racking, but really good and everyone really loved it."

As for the fans themselves, the Coopers/Kasabian line-up was a match made in heaven: here were two great bands for the price of one. Coopers fans suddenly had another set of songs to learn, another set of releases to collect, and another band to take to their hearts.

"There probably was a lot of crossovers in our fanbase," concedes Mahon, "which is great 'cause we were never out to keep all our fans to ourselves. It's great when you get that kind of cross-fertilisation and your fans really like the support act and the whole package that you're putting on. That's a really good thing, and I think the record company were clever putting us on together 'cause we clearly had some musical ties that complemented each other. They're a great live band and it was interesting to see them [develop]. When they started they were just kids really and we had just started a few years earlier than when they joined us on the road, which really matures you quickly in terms of performing and socialising."

As we shall soon see.

Even as the Kasabian name began to be known around the fringes of the mainstream, one of their demos found itself in the hands of a radio DJ whose own tastes spanned the gamut of musical styles, with a particular penchant for electronica. Eddy Temple-Morris was a fan of *good new music*, and he still is. His show on XFM reflected his tastes, and was seen as widely influential in often being the first port of call for those people who were interested in finding out first what new and exciting bands were up to. The first time he came across Kasabian was something of a fluke.

"There was this box in the XFM office," Eddy explained for this book, "where people who got CDs that they didn't want would throw them in. And every week I would basically go through the box and I would always find stuff there. Because there were so many indie-heads in XFM, they would often throw away anything electronic. There have been, over the years, a mass of tracks that have got on my show that weren't sent to me by anyone and I basically found them in the bin! I actively went through that box because I knew the taste of so many people at XFM, was really indie and *so* blinkered. I don't know who [the Kasabian demo] was sent to, but I found it. It was just basically two bits of cardboard with an elastic band in-between it, the 'Processed Beats' demo. It was just a blank CD-R, just said 'Kasabian', with one track on it, and it just blew me away. Blew me away completely and I just thought, 'This is great!' I played it the next week and then one thing led to another.

They are that type of band that inspires rabid devotion. They had it from me. The moment that I saw them I was completely in love with them and I would have done anything for them. I mean, the moment I heard that demo, I just thought, 'This band are fucking brilliant, I would put my dick on the chopping block for these boys.'" Temple-Morris was also DJ-ing in clubs around the country, as well as being heavily involved with a monthly night called *Kill All Hippies*, which is not only a splendid and intrinsically noble sentiment, but also a great night of top quality new bands performing, reflecting more than anything his XFM show itself.

"The next thing that happened," laughs the D.J., "is that I got collared at *Kill All Hippies* by Chris Karloff. *Kill All Hippies* started off as my birthday party and it went so well that it turned into a legendary monthly free club, it was such a laugh. And I would persuade bands to play for nothing and DJs to come and DJ for nothing. We'd regularly get eight hundred people coming up to see what was happening; it was a really cool thing. Chris was one of these people who was there right at the beginning of it. And he basically sort of slapped me on the back of that winding staircase and went, 'Oi, Eddy, my name's Chris, I'm in that band Kasabian. Thanks for your support, it really means a lot.' And that basically led to my getting them booked to play *Kill All Hippies*. It was only maybe a first band or a second band on. One of those legendary sort of 'I was there' support slots. There's probably eight thousand people now who say they were there and at the time there was only five hundred people *actually* there. I can pinpoint that as one of my favourite moments in my chequered career, of being somewhere special at a special time and *knowing* …

When you meet them and you see them play and see Serge and Tom [it's amazing]. Serge is knee-tremblingly good looking and Tom's got a great sort of Liam Gallagher swagger about him. The music was the human embodiment of what I was all about and what my show was all about. You know, dance rock. It's a rock band who you can play in a club and who I was playing in nightclubs, all over the place. Like I said, they're the kind of band that inspires almost religious devotion, like the Manic Street Preachers. The Movement was a clever way of galvanising all those people who would do anything for them and I was like a member of that Movement too. I was there, poised to play anything they gave me on the radio and to be there for them no matter what. And all of us, the other fans, were the same. [Even though at the time] they had no radio support apart from me, a little specialist show, and back then XFM was only on in London."

The support of someone like Eddy Temple-Morris at this stage of Kasabian's nascent career was a vital foothold in the music industry, particularly on the radio, which was as yet not hugely onboard with the band. The year 2003, however, had seen a huge jump ahead for the band both creatively and in terms of profile, but the following year was to prove an absolutely astonishing one.

CHAPTER ELEVEN

Some Stuff That Happened In Early 2004

2004 would begin with the band getting out and about once more, a couple of early January and February dates revving things up alongside the fact that one of the band's tracks, 'L.S.F. (Lost Souls Forever)' was garnering rather a lot of attention, not least because it was on the soundtrack for the successful football video game, 'Fifa 2004'. For a bunch of lads obsessed with both soccer and the PlayStation, there could have been no better start to the year. *The Fly* magazine, reviewing their Shepherd's Bush gig, was mightily impressed with this new musical force.

"Kasabian are undeniable heirs to the thrones of Oasis and the Primals' crumbled majesty," wrote the reviewer. "They're set to punctuate a whole new genre in British rock, and they believe it more than anyone." The magazine was particularly enamoured with what it called the "riotous beats and cinematic soundscapes" on offer.

Eddy Temple-Morris was up to his usual tricks, and Feburary 19, 2004 saw the group play the XFM Remix night at Cargo in London, this time alongside another group of electronic-obsessives, Cheltenham's artsy noisemakers Chikinki. Although Chikinki's fixation on the more esoteric aspects of electronic noisemaking made them a reasonable choice with whom to play, in reality the bands themselves shared very little in terms of actual musical aesthetics. Still, as favourites of Temple-Morris, and two bands tipped to rise quickly during the year, it was a rather exciting line-up, and the reviews of the night were very promising indeed.

"Playing quite creative punk rock borrowing the rolling bass of Black Rebel Motorcycle Club, the melodies of the Chemical Brothers and the vocal pattern of the Stone Roses," enthused a reviewer, "Kasabian had the crowd transfixed for a pitifully short half hour set."[34]

Chief cheerleader Eddy Temple-Morris recalls the excitement he felt on the night, watching his favourite new bands rip it up, as they had done the previous year at his own club night. "At the time and in retrospect, there were key moments. That *Kill All Hippies* gig and when they supported Chikinki at the XFM Remix night. This is before there was any support from XFM at all, apart from me. It was basically me and The Movement, and no one else. And I knew, each time, every evening that I saw that band, I just thought they blow everybody else away. They're the support band but they're blowing away the main bands and they've got something really special going on. I knew the same way that I knew that Gary Lightbody would be big one day when I first saw Snow Patrol, back when they'd just changed their name from Polar Bear and nobody gave a fuck. I had that feeling, that feeling of impending greatness that you get every now and then and it was really, really strong."

For the band's part, they were happy enough to be preparing for a year that was beginning to be booked solidly with gigs, including successful appearances supporting Black Rebel Motorcycle Club in February, whilst continuing to record where and when they could as they put the finishing touches to the Jacknife recordings with Jim Abbiss. Influential people, inspirational characters even, were also beginning to take notice of the Leicester boys, as Tom Meighan was to find out when he ran into one Liam Gallagher at Creation Records supreme Alan McGee's club, Death Disco at Kasabian's appearance there on February 18.

"You've got some bollocks," Gallagher told him. "You're a gang not a bunch of students. A proper band with a cool attitude. You're *rockin*."[35] Meighan was happy both to take the praise, whilst also finding the time to pronounce that, "There's nothing challenging the face of rock 'n' roll. It needs fucking with, and we're going to fuck with it,"[36] in one of the many magazine interviews with which the band were beginning to find their days filled. Chris Karloff, meanwhile, was typically coming across as a little more thoughtful – in an interview with *Clash Magazine*, he was somewhat dismissive of other bands whilst offering the magnificent epithet that Kasabian were, "white boys with big bollocks [playing] varied, harsh, dirty electronic rock rearranged."[37]

The next piece of vinyl to be released from its cage was another limited edition 10" single, the dark-but-powerful 'Reason Is Treason'. The 10" also contained a stencil of Kasabian Man, which coincidentally was suddenly being found sprayed in venues, on bridges, and lamp-posts, throughout the UK. Wonder who could have been responsible for that? 'Reason Is Treason' also spawned a very inventive video which was directed by Scott Lyon. It is a visual treat, with stock footage of riots and political events being doctored by the talented director.

"The budget for the video was tiny," Lyon exclusively recalls, "but I was really into the music – at that point there wasn't much around that sounded anything like that. Particularly because it had so much energy. I started to write some notes up and then met them in a pub in Islington for a chat about some ideas. The only kind of visual stuff that they had at that point was their logo with the guy in the mask [that] they were using as a backdrop to the shows they were doing. I got really inspired by that original image. It had this slightly anarchistic feel to it and went with my [idea] to get loads of news stock footage from various eras then basically sabotage it [by altering the images]. A lot of people have said it's quite political in certain bits, and although there was a thought toward that, it kind of wasn't. It was more of a piss-take, really. You've got city brokers and we put chickens' heads on them, and changed mobile phones for cucumbers and stuff like that – it was more about getting the images to fit with the music and also to create a kind of feeling of a visual image around the band that was a bit more 'out there', a bit more rebellious and a bit more anarchistic, I guess. I think it sums them up in a lot of ways; that idea of revolution is sort of carried on through all the videos in certain respects."

Although the final video has a hugely subversive and revolutionary feel, as Lyon says, it was as much about messing around with imagery as it was of any kind of call to arms, or mobilising of troops. It is, however, undeniably a visually arresting piece of work that belies the lack of available cash, proving – as the farm recordings themselves did – that it is *ideas* that are the important thing, and the execution thereof is down to technical skill.

"Because of the process of making videos," continues the director, "often you don't have very much time to do them, so it was more of a case of trawling through a load of library footage of stuff and coming across a load of interesting imagery, and then just thinking what you could do to it. There was a certain kind of political sense of it, 'cause once you get on a roll with things you start to see how certain images are working with each other and particularly as there's a lot of riot footage and some police brutality in certain elements, I definitely wanted to take the piss out of that. There's no doubt about it. So there are elements of that but we hadn't sat down and gone, 'Right, we want to do something that's really politically charged.' It wasn't really spoken, it was more about getting images that were really powerful and really drive the track, and then let's do something new to them – which was messing about with the context of what the image is and just kind of subverting it. My favourite shot in there is the flicknife [which] we replaced with a feather. Looking back, I thought that was a particularly fun image." The flicknife and the feather? Could be a Kasabian single title. Could be a *Stereophonics* single title.

Unusually for a group's debut video, it does not actually feature a single shot of the band themselves, which only added to the stealth mystique that was growing around Kasabian. "When they started off," continues Lyon, "they wanted there to be an element of mystery behind them. And they didn't go for what is probably traditionally the way to do the first music video, a straightforward band performance video in which they don't really spend much cash. Kind of *Our Band Are Called This And Here They Are*. It's so unnecessary, and there's so much more you can build up with a bit of mystique. It does all look the same, you see one of those performance videos back to back with another one and it's like a paint by numbers, 'Insert band here' type of idea. You don't have to have a band in a video for it to *be* that band and I think it's all about getting across what your ethos is, it's more of a statement to have your first video and not be in it. It is a very cinematic kind of track. We just went and did it, finished it, sent it off and everyone was happy with it and it went off. Sometimes there's a lot of to-ing and fro-ing for ages in videos where you have to take this shot out, put this shot in, but there wasn't with that. We heard everyone was happy and that was that."

"Having obviously consumed *XTRMNTR* with a bucketful of whatever drugs they can get their hands on," wrote respected reviewer Niall Doherty in *The Fly*, "Kasabian actually sound more Primal Scream than Primal Scream. Which is a total headfuck. Like the flux capacitor theory in *Back To The Future*."

Live-wise, things were hotting up tremendously, this time on tour with Chikinki. "We were both pretty much in the same position at the time," explained Trevor Wensley, one of that band's keyboardists, for this book. "We were both signed to big labels and had made a record and were about to start promoting it. At the time we were getting bits of press in *NME* and whatnot, so we kinda knew little bits about them. It was kinda odd 'cause the little snippets we'd seen, it was dirty beats and [we thought] that they were probably gonna be a bunch of rowdy football hooligans. That was the press angle that was going out at the time. And to be honest, they probably thought that we were some kind of electro sex-driven band where everything was slightly kinky, in the way that the press often pick up [on] these things and run with them for some reason. I remember we were driving off to the first gig in Norwich and all we'd heard was three [Kasabian] demo tunes, not the original recordings but demos, and someone went, 'Yeah, electro.' We're quite a synth-based band, and they'd use electronics more as effects but it was good stuff, all quite groove-based.

To start with, I think that we thought we'd have a lot in common musically but that we'd not have a lot in common, personally. But in the event it turned out the other way 'cause although there's a lot of similarities in the sounds and the electronic beats – 'cause we were using a live electric drumkit so the sounds were quite the same – the way we went about it was very different, 'cause we've never used any backing tracks or click tracks to play to. Kasabian's stuff, 'cause it's always been down to that four on the floor and the dance grooves, they've always been playing off a backing track with the drummer listening to it, so it's all quite set timewise, which means you always get it spot on and the tempo and the beat is predefined.

We're from quite different backgrounds, we'd all met at university and we were all a bit more arty in the way we went about making music and stuff and they were more about making a sound that was as much about 'aving it as possible – they were more to the point in that sense. So, I think, musically we were actually coming from quite different places but we crossed over in the type of the sounds that we were using and so they stuck us together. But we got on really well on that tour and the crowds really liked it."

The Movement were also firmly doing the business for their boys by this stage, too, which was not going unnoticed by Wensley and the Chikinki crew. "About halfway through the tour we'd be driving to gigs, trying to find the venue. We'd get a map and an address, and then you start noticing that on the lamppost there's arrows pointing to 'The Next Kasabian Event' that the street team had been putting out. You know, it obviously kicked in about halfway through where the marketing moved up a level. They had a great campaign with the posters and the artwork and everything. They got that spot on and that was obviously a big part of it, all hanging together and making sense and it all happened very quickly."

In fact, as had happened with the Cooper Temple Clause slots, fans would come to see both bands and more often than not leave as bigger fans of Kasabian than they were when they turned up. That's not to criticise Chikinki, who were, and who remain, a very inventive band. But by their own admission, they were less unashamedly populist as Kasabian were becoming, and with the infectious energy of their live set, the Leicester boys were certainly steaming ahead at full force.

The tour was also unique for its rotating headline spot. "We were doing a joint headline thing," explains Wensley. "So we'd take turns each night as to who went on last, depending in which city we were. In the end they just kept adding more dates 'cause it grew and grew. The crowds kept getting better and better 'cause we were getting more and more press at the time, we both were, and it grew from there. It made for a really good gig. What made it better as well was that because we had that competitive edge of who was gonna go on last, taking turns as to who would be the headline and who would be the support act, we'd play off each other in that sense. Everyone wants to be the headline act, the best band of the night, so you'd want to blow the other band offstage and that pushed everyone a bit further as well. So it was a good little tour in that sense.

The way we went about making music, writing songs, was quite different. For us, it was much more of a five-way thing, playing off each other and making up different ideas, whilst for them it was more about creating a sound and, I think, Serge trying to make certain riffs and tracks, more riffs and grooves, and trying to build off that. Tom sings completely different to Rupert, our singer, you know. A different kind of frontman, but both great frontmen so it was a great fiery kind of thing. It was an exciting tour, especially 'cause it was new for us all and neither of us knew what was going to happen. And we were both in the slightly fragile position of having signed with a major but not knowing whether they were really going to run with it or not."

If the cash was still a little short, the fun aspect was higher than ever. Phil Bunford recalls playing as support to Chikinki and Kasabian at a gig in Birmingham's Jug Of Ale venue. Phil's band at the time were called My Dad Hitla, which is a brilliant name for a band, and it's truly tragic that they've subsequently split up.

"I'd never heard of them to be honest," Bunford told me, "cause they were just another band to play with at the time. The audience reaction was really good for Kasabian, they must have brought around a hundred people with them 'cause the place was rammed and a lot of them watched all the bands, but when Kasabian came on it was like they were playing to their home crowd. It was very busy. The thing I remember was people not so much jumping up and down but *dancing* to them. We were in-your-face, punky style, but Kasabian were quite funky, people obviously knew the tunes and were having a dance to them. I thought they were pretty good, there were three or four songs that hit me immediately and it just clicked from there, they just started getting bigger and bigger. You could tell that they were no slouches or anything. Tom, I remember, had this crazy jacket on when we were setting up, like Doctor Who or Joseph And His Technicolour Dreamcoat! I remember seeing that, and Serge was asking how we got our band name. Tom's a really nice guy, he had a lot of charisma. He didn't have the greatest singing voice in the world, but he was carrying it with his charisma."

"I remember the gig well," says Arthur Tapp, who promoted said shindig. "It was a mental one – all their mates piled over from Leicester and tried to get in free through the fire escape, so I spent most of the show with a bunch of lads shouting, 'Open the fire escape, cunt!' through the window. Nice fans. The band were great though. Tom spent all night talking me to death about football and I think it took us an hour to get them to leave 'cause they wouldn't stop talking. Then Tom sat cross-legged in the car park for half an hour. Lovely guys and a sold out gig – but didn't like their fans much. They put those Kasabian Event road signs all round Moseley which were really cool as well."

With the tour rumbling around the country, Ryan Glover was enjoying himself behind the kit, even if it was having a few odd effects on his physiognomy.

"It's the same for any band, it's very tough to spread the word around," he says. "You've got to have the right songs 'cause at the end of the day if you've got the songs, you're gonna go somewhere. I knew the band were gonna make it and be relatively big because of the songs they had. It had that kind of Northern swagger to it because of the influences that they had from Oasis and stuff, but at the same time they had that edge, that attitude and that rawness that they carried it off live. It was really weird, 'cause after the tour, I got into the habit of hitting the drums really hard. I used to come back off tour, and I used to lose a load of weight around my stomach so I used to look really ill and stick-thin – but my arms were *huge*! I used to look really strange. I just used to love smashing the crap out of the kit for those guys. Even if there was just one man and his dog, I'd still bash seven bells of shit out of the kit 'cause that's what I loved doing. That's what I'm about.

It was really, really good fun, good times at that point. Kasabian had a massive fanbase from the start, I met a lot of their old college friends, schoolfriends, friends and family on part of the tour. At one particular gig in Coventry, they had a whole bus-load of the old football fans, people they used to go to the football with. Complete bunch of nutters who were singing loads of football songs throughout the gig – it was awesome, really, really good to hear. They had quite a big following anyway, a lot of people who would travel quite far round the country to see them.

To put it into my perspective, at the end of the day, as much as I was involved with the band and they were really nice to me and really good to me, I was just a kid from Pompey playing drums for them. I didn't kind of *feel* it as much as those guys did, 'cause those guys were with people they had known for years, whereas I hadn't. Whenever I met the people at a gig, the friends, family and management, it was new faces all the time whereas all those guys had been together so many years and known their friends for some many years. They were feeling it so much more than I was."

Ryan was also fitting in the odd recording session with the band, and even if he did occasionally feel the dislocation he mentions, from the core centre of Team Kasabian he had also picked up a nickname, 'Sixties Killer', which came from a typically lateral piece of thinking from Tom Meighan.

"The Sixties Killer thing," laughs the drummer, "is just something Tom came out with when I went up to the farm one time after buying a load of clothes ready for the next few weeks of gigging and stuff. One particular top I was wearing caught Tom's eye, and he just stood there with Serge and said I looked like some sort of Sixties killer, 'cause my hair was growing long and the clothes I'd bought were very retro sorta Sixties or Seventies, and along with the Buddy

Holly-style glasses I wear I s'pose I could see his point." Welcome to the Family …

One of the more prosaic reasons that the band were becoming so popular, too, was that they would take every opportunity possible to talk to journalists. The Leicester (and Pompey) lads understood that although it was one hell of a ride, one hell of a laugh, and one hell of a party, there was still work to do. This hugely impressive work ethic and genuine willingness to accommodate interviewers is actually something that is sometimes overlooked when people talk about the band's liking for what they call 'Getting Big', or getting in the zone.

"Every gig on the tours," explains Ryan Glover, "there was somebody from some magazine somewhere that had to interview us, whether it be a student one or some sort of local magazine. There was a general kind of 'calm before the storm' feeling – people were getting to know about it, people were spreading the word and there was talk of this great band that were going around, but at the same time, 'cause we weren't doing loads and loads of gigs everywhere straight away, it was kind of our little thing and we still had to put in the great performances in for the people who had been there from the start."

And the performances were almost uniformly great, with the band nailing it, night after night after night, the 'rotating headliner' aspect becoming rather more of a conceptual profile-sharing. In reality, it was Kasabian whose stock was growing the fastest.

"It was really funny watching the fans," says soundman Acky Hannis. "They both have electronic influences, but they're [different]. You could tell, straight away, who people were there to see, instantly, as soon as you walked in the room. As a unit, it was a well-oiled machine. Evil Dave tour managed and his friend Dan came in for a while as well. They do love playing, they are happiest when they're on the road. When they weren't, they were standing around on the farm getting bored, they need to be out doing something, drawing attention and out there doing it.

They were solid, I think I probably saw two bad gigs, but a bad gig in the sense of us playing was, 'Oh shit, we had a bum note there,' or the vibe wasn't quite right, but nine and a half times out of ten we had a solid performance. They were so consistent in the shows, even when they thought they had a bad show I'd recorded it and they hadn't – everything about them was so *consistent* and that goes back to day one. Obviously it was rougher round the edges but that's why I went on the road with them 'cause I only tour with bands I actually like."

The tour also saw the odd hairy moment, some of which, in retrospect were downright hazardous. Rock 'n' roll is meant to be a bit dangerous, of course, but occasionally things were rather less than angelic for the motley crew.

"It's partly the fact that you're given a free rein," explains Trevor Wensley of his experiences on that tour. "And it's also a fact that you feel that you're expected to do certain things 'cause the bands you admire [do it]. It's all part of the mythology of being in a band, when things go a bit messy with drink or drugs or just in a 'girls everywhere' kind of way. It is amazing what difference a bit of press can make to the amount of female attention you get. That's one of the surprising things I noticed after we were getting a couple of mentions in the *NME* or something, is that people will turn up on that basis and girls will be interested in you just 'cause of that. It's quite a strange transition."[38]

The band themselves were still skint, and inevitably this meant that the van they'd travel around in was prone to the odd bout of temperament. On one particular occasion, it had given up the ghost somewhat after a gig at King Tut's Wah-Wah Hut up in Glasgow, which if you've ever been lucky enough to visit, is a very hilly city indeed. No problem, at least not according to Acky Hanning.

"We both had splitter vans at the top of this hill," chuckles Trevor Wensley. "And their sound engineer decides that if he just rolls it down the hill, he could jump start it. He gets in, we're all … going, 'Yeeeah what a great idea' and just as we're setting off someone goes, 'But aren't the brakes power assisted? You need to turn the engine on before they work!' So there was this frozen moment where we were imagining getting to the bottom and smashing through lines of traffic before we stopped, 'cause he wouldn't be able to turn the brakes on but thankfully the power kicked in at the last minute and he did. But you kind of let things like that pass you by at the time because there's just this general encouragement that it's all a bit slapdash and it'll all somehow just hang together in the end."

Put simply, everyone was having a ball. Rupert Browne, lead singer with Chikinki, was pleased that the general atmosphere was conducive not only to the odd hair-raising moment but also that fun was nearly always guaranteed when hanging out with Kasabian. He speaks highly of the band, not least their singer.

"Tom's such a lovely guy," Browne told me. "He's really nice and spends the whole time making sure everyone's happy and having a good time and not taking themselves too seriously or anything. He's really great like that. The others are quite quiet, quite shy in a way when we were on tour with them. But Tom's just running around, saying, 'Heyyyy, isn't it great?! How are you doing?!' With Kasabian it was ... stable, you felt like everything was really easy and they were very professional.

I think they've probably got a lot more rock 'n' roll, 'cause as the tour went along they started staying out later and stuff. When we started, they were really quite broke, they had completely spent all the advance and everything whereas we were still alright. They are really professional, they always get to the show on time, they always soundcheck properly and they always play a really good show all night."

As the tour came to its climax, there were two final gigs: one in Birmingham, and the next night, the final show, down in Southampton. As things turned out, however, the Southampton concert was notable for Kasabian's absence, which was apparently down to that pesky van breaking down once more.

"I talked to their tour manager at the time, Evil Dave," remembers Movement member Amanda McGowan. "He'd call me every day and literally say, 'Can you come here? Can you do this [for us]?, Can you do that?' and he sent me a message saying the bus had broken down, and he asked if I was in Southampton. I said, 'Yes, I am actually,' and he said, 'Cool, can you go down there and tell everyone we've broken down?'. I said, 'Yeah, okay.'"

Which presented a couple of problems, not least that there was a crowd there who were expecting to see both Chikinki and Kasabian. What to do?

"We were conscious of there being Kasabian fans there," continues Browne, "so we thought, 'Let's do a cover,' and 'Processed Beats' seemed to be the obvious one to do. We listened to it in the van and I phoned up one of the guys, trying to check the lyrics 'cause some of their lyrics are a bit barmy. I said, 'I'm worried it won't make sense,' and they said, 'Just sing anything, it doesn't matter!' It was great, there were a couple of people who were only there to see Kasabian who were like, 'Play that one again!' and it was nice. It was a good gig, Southampton was a place where it was more our crowd than Kasabian's, so it's not like there was gonna be a riot with them not turning up. We worked it out in the van, did it a couple of times in the soundcheck, and it was really rough and ready. I got a couple of the lyrics wrong and stuff, but it's one of those songs where if you get the right beat with it, it's all jammy anyway, so you can have a bit of fun with it."

It has become one of the legendary performances in recent rock history as a result, and shows the camaraderie that the bands had developed over the course of their touring together. It was a sweet moment in many ways, but that Southampton non-appearance was poignant for Ryan Glover, who had been looking forward to it for months.

"The van actually broke down in Leicester, which is sod's law," he sighs, "cause we were due to play in my technically home town [of Southampton], and we had to cancel the gig, I went home[39]. I remember distinctly saying at the time to Serge and Chris Karloff, 'Give us a call when you get back and let me know how it goes, I'll be here waiting, have a good time,' saying my goodbyes and all the rest of it." As it turns out, he was to be waiting for rather a long time …

CHAPTER TWELVE

Brother, Can You Spare A Dime?

You could more than forgive Kasabian feeling that everything was coming up roses for them: reviews and interviews were, without exception, positive, Liam Gallagher was pronouncing them the best thing to hit music since, well, Oasis, and the gigs kept coming thick and fast. The album (at this stage with the working title of *Test Transmission*) was gelling very nicely with Jim Abbiss and Barny, and the group were preparing to put out another piece of vinyl, the insistent 'Club Foot'. To that end, a video shoot was organised with Wiz, the hugely talented video director who had worked with many luminaries in the music industry: Chemical Brothers, Ian Brown, Manic Street Preachers, Happy Mondays etc. The 'Club Foot' shoot was to take place in Budapest on March 11, 2004, with a storyboard involving the band playing in a disused Russian Army camp, whilst cult Russian actress Dinara Drukarova variously hid from and then faced down the incoming tanks, echoing that famous student in Tianamen Square. It was an ambitious and cinematic concept, more a short film than a traditional music video, and the black and white ambience and tumbledown Eastern European modern architecture only added to the mystique and revolutionary feel surrounding the band.

So far, so good, but the problem was that one member was missing: Ryan Glover, who had been left behind in Southampton, without a passport to his name and with a mounting sense that whilst life in the band was excellent and enjoyable, Practically he was finding it extremely hard.

Ryan not having a passport also presented something of an immediate problem, what with the group on the verge of flying out to Budapest to shoot the video which was to push them even further into the musical consciousness of the nation. The solution? Well, Ryan had an elder brother, didn't he? And he was also something of a talented drummer, too. Re-enter Mitch on his white horse to save the day.

"I jumped in at the deep end," recalls Mitch, "and did the video and then a load of gigs with the band. They called me and woke me up at about six in the morning, and I was at the airport by midday so it was all a bit weird! Then here was the second chance for me to join the band."

Ryan Glover says in retrospect that it was a shame that the communication broke down between the band, himself and the management, but his time with Kasabian was a productive one for all concerned. He bears no grudges toward the band themselves, and is in fact still heavily involved with music, currently drumming for the very talented new artist, Mark Rooney.

With Mitch temporarily filling in on the drum stool, Kasabian steadied the ship at a very, very crucial time for all concerned. The 'Club Foot' video was going down to almost universal acclaim, and later Wiz dedicated his impressive piece of work to the Czech freedom fighter, Jan Palach.

A couple of gigs with American act Von Bondies saw the band through April successfully, leading up to the release of 'Club Foot' on May 10, 2004. It stormed into the charts, reaching Number 19 in the UK. This was the first charting single by the band, and to go in at that relatively high level was testament indeed to the hard work put in behind the scenes as much as it was from the group's constant onstage triumphs. Of the single, Serge called it, "a big sound, it's euphoric."

Tom Meighan agreed: "Yeah, it's just about getting down. We know we're all fucked, so let's get down before we all die! We're just here to play our tunes and bang, there it is – plug it in, do your gig and get fucked. That's a rock and roll show – it's all about that feeling!" A fine sentiment, indeed. Meighan also expanded on the raison d'etre of the group, whose career had taken shape during the altered-state worldview that followed the attacks on the World Trade Center on September 11, 2001. He spoke of the paranoia and lethargy that had developed as a result, and called for a very specific type of mobilisation.

Tom rips it up on stage.
Photo courtesy of Fiona McKinlay

When we were young: ultra-rare shot of Tom, Serge and Alan Rawlings
laying down Saracuse tracks in Bedrock Studios.
Photo courtesy of Scott Gilbert

Killing Hippies with Eddy Temple-Morris at the
famous Fortress Studios gig, Old Street, London.
Photo courtesy of Heike Schneider-Matzigkeit

Calm before the storm: Chris Karloff and Serge Pizzorno relaxed and
happy backstage at Middlesbrough, on tour with Chikinki, February 2004.
Photo courtesy of Amanda McGowan

Come 'ere gorgeous: Tom and Serge share a special moment,
Summer Sonic Festival, August 2004.
Photo courtesy of Rumi Oyama

Tom gets the Gary Lineker treatment in Japan, November 2004.
Photo courtesy of Rumi Oyama

Serge shows Leicester City how it's done, backstage
at 0$_2$ Wireless Festival, 2005.
Photo courtesy of Alex Sudea/Rex Features

Serge dripping with cool at Across The Narrows Festival,
New York, October, 2005.
Photo courtesy of Rumi Oyama

Tom practises his bowls moves whilst Dibs looks
on appreciatively, at Across The Narrows Festival.
Photo courtesy of Rumi Oyama

And then there were four ... Kasabian at an in-store appearance for
the *Empire* album, August 30, 2006.
Photo courtesy of Hugh Thompson/Rex Features

"I did it myyyyy wayyyyy!" Tom and Andy Stone of
The Displacements sharing a stage at a family wedding, 2006.
Photo courtesy of Andy Stone

Tom guesting onstage with The Displacements at the
same wedding, 2006.
Photo courtesy of Andy Stone

Tom indicating what number the band's record has reached at the
Q awards, October 30, 2006.
Photo courtesy of Brian Rasic/Rex Features

Shooting for the stars at Live Earth, Wembley, July 7, 2007.
Photo courtesy of David Fisher/Rex Features

'Aving it onstage at Somerset House, July 13, 2007.
Photo courtesy of Michelle Brooks www.michellebrooks.co.uk

"We just want kids back on the park, that's a big one. They're too scared to go out. We're fed up of seeing kids like zombies, texting each other every five minutes, or playing on their PlayStations and not playing in the park. That pisses us off … It's as simple as that. It's not like we want to blow down the Houses of Parliament – there are others that want to do that, as we are reminded every fucking day. It's everyday life we want to change."

'Club Foot' was well-received itself, but possibly just as welcome was the 'vocal mix' remix constructed by the excitingly skilful Jagz Kooner, who had worked with a vast amount of groups from Manic Street Preachers and Radio 4 to Massive Attack, Rammstein and Primal Scream.

"Basically they just sent me the instrumental, the *a cappella*," he told me. "I just built up a whole new backing track around [that]. There's no one set way of doing a remix. You might hear a tune somewhere and go, 'Ah, I think I know what I want to with that.' But you might actually get into a studio to start doing it and you might hear something that you didn't hear before and it's like, bang! You're just off on a [different] tangent completely.

It did them a favour and it did me a favour really. It was a great tune; the chorus is catchy as fuck. But I think it actually kind of helped them in certain ways, because I think for a while Radio One really dug the remix I did. I think Zane Lowe played it, Jo Whiley played it and Annie Mac was on it as well. So, I think it kind of opened a few doors at Radio One for them as well and it all added to the cause; when 'Club Foot' actually came out, I don't think Radio One even playlisted it. I think Radio One only playlisted it *after* it had gone into the charts, then it was like Radio One said, 'Oh there's this great new band we've discovered.' You know, 'Of course you have, they're in the fucking charts, you have to play them now!' sort of thing. But it was essentially the fanbase that got them into the charts and that's just amazing, that's brilliant. Just by going around playing pubs and clubs and stuff and building up that loyal following. It just goes to show you get that fanbase in place and it makes a world of difference."

The band's summer schedule leading up to the release of the debut album was full, of course, including appearances at all the major festivals (as well as the final gig/party/festival at the farm during May, which was videoed for posterity as 'Field Of Dreams'). Along with the growing buzz round 'Club Foot', it would all give Kasabian the triple whammy of credibility that they could provide a

great, band-based live experience, whilst being part of the creation
of neo-revolutionary, semi-political short films, and also having damn
danceable tunes that could rip up the dancefloor in the clubs. There
had been very, very few bands over the years with the ability to do
that and to cross over between rock and dance with quite so much
aplomb. The press, quite frankly, were a little bemused: the last people
to do it were from the so-called 'baggy' movement of the late
Eighties, that is, Stone Roses, Happy Mondays, and to a lesser extent
The Farm and others. And whilst, quite clearly, Kasabian's energetic,
almost punk rock assault was a lot harder edged than their
predecessors, it would be those bands who would be often
referenced by journalists who were scurrying around to try and
make sense of this new phenomenon in terms that they already
understood. There was an element of truth in the baggy reference,
but only in the same way that, because the band sometimes used
distorted and sometimes psychedelic guitars, they were therefore
major Hendrix acolytes.

"The thing with the baggy thing is what I don't get," sighed Tom
Meighan to journalist Matt Cartmell. "It's 'cause the Happy
Mondays used beats, they were a dance band, it was in that wave at
the beginning of the Nineties. It was in that acid house thing. I don't
really get the comparison with the Mondays to be honest. The thing
is the attitude. That's the main thing. People have said Oasis, they've
said Stone Roses and the Mondays, but I think it's the attitude that
we don't give a fuck. And it's as simple as that."

On the other hand, behind the confidence and the public
pronouncements, the band were still the down-to-earth Leicester
lads they always had been. James Milton-Thompson, one of the
original Movement members, recalls a particular evening spent in the
always stimulating company of the band.

"You saw the confidence growing, you saw the venues getting
bigger and you saw them getting more [confident]. It was quite
special, really. I went over to Paris and saw them, it was just me, my
mate Trevor and the band sat in a bar at 3am chatting about how it'd
gone over the year. It's just great memories, really. They couldn't
believe it, they were saying, 'This is stupid, we've got a year ahead of
us playing all these festivals, all these big venues, we just can't believe
it.' Tom's jokey, 'We're gonna be massive, we're brilliant,' to the
cameras he's cocky, like Noel Gallagher sort of thing but to your
face, secretly, he's like, 'Oh, you know … I don't know how we've
done it, we're crap really but we've made it!' Going to the gigs, in a

strange way, it was like going to the football, following your team. The passion for it, you just went to the gig, whether it's in Coventry or Liverpool or wherever, you've just gotta go. You'd follow them round the whole country. They had their regulars with them, us, everyone, their troops following them.

It literally upturned British music. It was dead, Britpop, and it basically just brought it alive again. Guitar music, anyway. You had all the garage rock and the punk funk and all that, which had died out. The Strokes and The White Stripes had been and gone, and then Kasabian just changed it all completely. It was the specialness of it – like a secret little thing. You go off, you see the band, you chat with them. It was changing the face of music in the UK, completely upturning it. Just the attitude, nobody had had that in ten years since Oasis. It's so fun to be part of, but you could easily miss out on it, just a few months and then they're big and that's it. But if you catch a band and see them from the start you know from the moment you see them that they're going to be unbelievable."

Something else that was pretty unbelievable was the fact that Kasabian had been chosen to support none other than British rock behemoths The Who, on a couple of dates. The gigs, at Birmingham NEC on June 7 and Cardiff International Arena on June 11, were an astonishing glimpse into the brightest light for the band.

"The management just rang us up and said, y'know, 'The Who want to play with you,'" revealed Chris Edwards. "And we were just, 'Err, okay.' I don't think we believed it at the start, actually, since we told our management 'bollocks'. But those gigs were a completely new experience for us."[40]

Huge gigs aside, Kasabian were keeping up the truly underground vibe, quite literally as it turned out, as they put on what was known as a 'guerrilla gig' at none other than the Cabinet War Rooms in London, on June 15, 2004. Essentially, this is a secret gig that the fans only found out about at the very last minute. It was typical of the group's sense of humour and sense of the legendary that they would pick such a venue, being the underground cavern from which Winston Churchill often directed events during World War II. It was an invited audience of competition winners and fans. *Dirty Zine*'s Ollie Connors was there.

"The whole operation was tight, to say the least. Guards at the door, armed only with a guestlist. If your name wasn't down, you weren't going in. The stairs leading down looked like [they were] leading into the abyss. It got darker and scarier. There was, however, light at the end of the tunnel. The bunker was as dusty as it was smelly. There were pictures of the Queen and Winston Churchill on the walls, with Kasabian stickers over the faces. Finally, at around eight, the band we had come to see took the stage, beginning their set with, 'We were gonna play an underground station, but apparently there's a strike or summat.'"[41]

"Arriving onstage to a rapturous reception," reported NME.com, "the band's set included singles 'Club Foot', which went into the Top 20, 'Reason Is Treason' and 'Processed Beats', as well as live favourite '55' and forthcoming single 'L.S.F.'"

A pivotal moment for the group was to soon present itself: opening The Other Stage at Glastonbury, on Friday June 25, 2004. It's the pinnacle of many bands' careers to play the festival at all, but to effectively kick off the party was tailor-made for the Leicester boys, who rolled up at the gates after a typically ebullient night of partying.

"We were playing in Newport, the day before Glastonbury," says Jersey Budd, fellow Leicestershire musician, rightly tipped for great things in his own right and who at the time was also billed for a Glasto appearance. "I was playing before Kasabian, then I went up for the last song, Tom brought me on for 'L.S.F.' and it was fucking incredible. Then we had a bit of a smash-up at the hotel! They were playing on the Friday as well so [they said], 'We're going in, we'll give you a lift on the tour bus.' So it was all going well but then a few people were late, the roads were blocked up, they wouldn't let us through so I missed my slot at Glastonbury, but we watched the boys!"

The significance of the Glastonbury appearance, which twenty thousand people watched at 11am, was not lost on Kasabian: this is a band who, even in their previous incarnations, had always envisaged themselves on such a high profile stage.

"When we walked out on stage and saw those people, it was like, 'Jesus, we've done something here,'" Serge told Hannah Hamilton. "The music we're making and the things we're saying, people are getting it. At band practice, like six years ago, Tom would scream, 'Glastonbury!' at a certain point during a song and, when we were on stage there, he said the same thing. It took me back to being that kid that was in that practice room with the carpet on the walls, dreaming of being in a band, and it was all happening to me now. That kid is important. I'm always going to remember him. It's easy to forget when all this shit goes off. That naive and optimistic kid has got to stay in my body."

The naivety and optimism was in full flow at the festival, for sure. Serge was famously approached by supermodel Kate Moss, well known as a 'friend' of various rock stars. As rumour had it, she was very interested in this shy, intelligent, mysterious and talented Leicester songwriter in front of her. As legend equally has it, Pizzorno turned down the chance to take things further with La Moss.

"At the time," explains Rupert Browne of Chikinki, whose band was also playing the 2004 summer festivals, "they all had girlfriends and they were all quite sensible with that sort of stuff [and] at one point Serge turned down Kate Moss. We got told it by the band!"

The reality, however, was perhaps a lot more prosaic, Serge admitting to the *Daily Record* later that, "Yes, I was with her. But I was a bit out of it at the time so I didn't know if I was up or down. It was a bit of an insane time for me to have realised a dream I've had since I was a kid. There she was sitting around a campfire and invited me to go for a drink there and then. The story has snowballed since then but nothing happened."[43]

Tom Meighan was excited by the band's triumphant appearance, commenting that although they had previously been to V and Reading Festivals, this was the first time any of the group had attended Glastonbury.

"Everyone just vibes with each other, so to be playing and truly become a part of it all is amazing. It's what we're all about. Glastonbury is a huge part of the British music scene. It's got a magic, a mystique – it's almost telepathic. For one weekend, everyone seems to tune into each other. That's a very special thing." He also revealed that the band would be staying for the whole of the rest of the weekend, "depending on how monged we get."[44]

The opening slot had been filled the previous year by 'flavour of the month' ludicrous, spandex rock, is-it-a-joke-or-not The Darkness, who had been one of the bands in the firing line of the increasingly sharp-tongued group.

"I just heard [Tom] say something on the mic," revealed Serge to Matt Cartmell, "and the feedback he got, it was like, Jesus Christ! Amazing. Absolutely brilliant. We got more than them bastards as well! But they're alright. When they came out I kind of slagged them, but I was pretty stoned in the day and I listened to them and I actually thought it was very funny. And then we all started singing ['I Believe In A Thing Called Love'] to each other. But I feel sorry for the guy, because I saw him backstage at T In The Park, and when you see [respected] people who are kind of in the music scene, and you walk by and they go, 'There's that guy that wrote that tune,' and everyone's got this kind of respect for him, but this guy [Darkness singer, Justin Hawkins] walks past and everyone's *laughing*. It must get to you a bit because they are comedians. It's a strange place to be."[45] "The British charts have always been dominated by comedy acts. We used to have The Wurzels, and The Darkness can easily be compared to somebody like that."[46]

One thing you could never accuse Kasabian of was being boring interviewees. They were also in full flow in *Bullitt* magazine the same month. "What have The Distillers got to do with rock 'n' roll?" raged Meighan. "Fuck all … it's like The Vines. That Craig Nicholls thinks he's cool as fuck and he just wants a smack in the head. It's just lame as fuck, boring."[47] Clearly, Kasabian were a band on a mission to change things for the better.

The band were asked by *NME* to play in their influential tent at the V Festival, and then headlined the Carling New Bands stage at the Reading and Leeds Festivals, providing another bump in popularity as the heat of the summer intensified in every way. Simply put, Kasabian were building up such momentum that they were beginning to look unstoppable.

"They're on blistering form, cutting dark beats with gram-loads of punk fury," wrote a reviewer for XFM. "The audience knows this is the best excuse going for hedonism, and crowd members form human climbing frames for gurning sweat monsters. Less active onlookers are openly ridiculed. It's unclear whether some people are dancing or fighting. As the band tear through the psychedelic fury of 'Club Foot' we nearly black out with activity, and set closer 'L.S.F.' has arms aloft all around the tent."[48].

By the time that the group released 'L.S.F.' as a single, on August 9, 2004, there was an almost unbearable wave of sheer excitement from press and fans alike. "'L.S.F.', to me, is a Motown tune," explained Serge to Hannah Hamilton in an interview for *Play Music*. "With a big orchestra and a big chorus. That's something that's definitely lacking in music in general – pop songs and music that connects with people. Bands are too scared to do it because they think it's uncool, or they hide behind the fact that they can't do it so they just make really strange music that no-one really gets. Or they do something generic that's been heard a million times before."

The year was hotting up, and Eddy Temple-Morris was fighting the group's corner in radio-land as best he could. Frustrated that his bosses weren't as enamoured of the band as he was, the DJ was waging a campaign of attrition to try and get Kasabian playlisted on the radio station.

"I remember DJing at Cargo and dropping 'Reason is Treason' there for the first time and I remember the audible *whoompf* from the dancefloor when those beats started in the mix of something else. When that backing vocal starts, literally, hands started going up in the air and people started screaming towards the DJ booth. And I started feeding that back, really proper club-based feedback, to the Head of Music. I couldn't get any more immediate, direct feedback than that. And the silence was deafening. Not even an 'Okay, thanks for the tip' [came] back. So, next time I saw him at XFM, I basically barrelled up to him, not threatening, but I just threw my hands in the air and went, 'What is your problem with Kasabian? Have they done something nasty to you or something?' This is after me and the Movement have got them into the [charts] and they've had not one single play from XFM. I was like, 'Did they eat your hamster when you were a kid, what is your problem?' And he just looked at me and went 'Eddy, I just hate them.'

He goes, 'It's all hype. Record company hype. Don't believe the hype.' And I said, 'I'm there in the clubs listening to the whoops of joy when I fucking drop that record. And that happens from Land's End to John O'Groats, man. We got them into the charts, right, me and their fans got them into the [charts]. If it was hype how the fuck aren't the Cooper Temple Clause in the [charts] then? You know, you're talking crap, you're talking absolute crap.' So then he goes, 'Oh, you know, they've got no tunes. Maybe 'L.S.F', the next single's going to be 'L.S.F'. Maybe we can support that.'"

Which the station eventually did, after much badgering from Temple-Morris and campaigning from The Movement alike, as the single itself crashed into the charts, reaching Number Ten, which was no mean feat for a band that had begun the year as an interesting tip for those in the know and a denouement of sorts for the hard work that had been put into the last two years or thereabouts.

"That was just from people buying music who had come to our gigs," said Serge. "We'd been on the road for two years playing loads of little towns all over the country. It was just through hard work that we got that chart position. It wasn't from over-hype in the media and it wasn't because we were all over the radio, 'cause we weren't. We just played these shows, loads of shows, and we made them count, y'know, every show we did, whether it be in Shrewsbury or Stoke or

Ipswich, we gave them everything we had and they remembered us for it."[49]

There was also the little matter that the song was an extremely good pop record, as Nick Raymonde explains. "'Club Foot' was just a hit record. You knew it was. I don't think there's anything particularly insightful about A&R; you just have to have a feeling about what other people would like, and I think we all do that, don't we? When everyone heard 'Club Foot', they said, 'That sounds like a hit record.'"

And it was.

As Eddy Temple-Morris says, too, 'The good will out.'

Or to be completely exact, it was time for The Album To Out ...

CHAPTER THIRTEEN

Steaks And CDs

"We get quite bored quite easily," declares Serge Pizzorno, "and when we've listened to the track a few times it's like, 'Let's put that bit in there.' Usually, it'll be by chance. If you're working with a loop for a long time, you suddenly hear what should be there. We really take care in where everything's placed in the music. We take a lot of time on each song."[(50)]

But now the time to stop obsessing about the nooks and the crannies had come: after all the problems, set-backs, repositionings and reworkings of their material, it was time to nail the colours to the mast and let the self-titled debut album breathe and blast on its own merits.

"The production side's the most important," says Tom Meighan. "Every song on the album you could play on a piano or acoustic and people would still get into it, but the clever part is to then add strange sounds, you know, so you can listen to it more than once. [And] not the same kind of guitar sound that everyone else is using. The earliest track on here is 'Processed Beats'. That kind of kicked us all off into getting that big attacking drum sound, that dance boogie sound. Big Beats, it started from there really."

That track was not only the debut single, but the first time that the band had truly moved into more experimental, groove-based territory. The skeleton of it was recorded in Bink Bonk studios with Mat Sampson and a session drummer by the name of Ian Matthews, who was well known on the Bristol circuit as a gentleman, scholar and damned fine sticksman to boot. A little older than the Kasabian crew, he'd inputted also onto album track, 'Butcher Blues', which was in its earliest stages known by the name of 'Omnichord'. Step forward Chris Karloff, Jim Pratt, Ben Cole and the process of sticking knives into the back of squealing keyboards! With Mitch Glover's Kosheen commitments, Kasabian had also been searching far and wide for a full-time tubthumper, although there was already a talented one closer to hand than they might think.

"We auditioned like fuck for a while," laughs soundman Ash Hannis. "I remember being in The Courtyard in south Putney for two weeks solid, constantly bringing these drummers in from agencies and they were all utter shite! I was actually stood there laughing my brains out from behind the mixing desk. It's a weird rehearsal room, you've got the Spice Girls' set-up, a massive mirrored room and you've actually got a full P.A. set-up. I was like, 'Bloody hell, guys!' I think at that point they didn't know I played drums so it was hilarious. I got up with the bass player Chris and started jamming and they were like, 'Bloody hell!' 'cause I knew the set inside out by that point. All the drummers they'd auditioned were fucking *terrible* to be honest. It was such a good laugh with them. I didn't do any gigs with them, just a bit of a jam and it was quite a lot of fun, 'cause by that point I must have mixed them probably a couple of hundred times and I probably knew the set better than they did! It was fantastic."

Hannis was never going to be a member of the band, however, his talents being equally if not better served behind the mixing desk. So it was eventually decided that Ian Matthews would be the latest incumbent of the kit.

"Ian has incredible bright, shiny eyes, full of light and mischievousness," reveals Jo Swan, vocalist in the band Ilya, of which Matthews was previously part. "Ian has immaculate gentlemanly manners and a downright filthy sense of humour! Because Ian wants to please and be liked, he is predisposed to fit in very well with any band. He is born to it. He was put on earth to play the drums! I remember Ian coming in to put drums on a track ... he was really grumpy and pissed off but the minute he got behind the kit and started playing he transformed mentally and physically, he became happy and relaxed and free from his nagging mind. He is an extremely handsome drummer and an absolute joy to watch because he just lets go and plays with wild abandon and a huge grin, while being totally on the ball, receptive to all the musicians and letting out this powerhouse of a sound!" High praise indeed. Matthews had been a sessionist in and around Bristol for a number of years, working with many talented musicians, including the ultra-talented jazz trumpet player John Hoare on many occasions.

"We were playing in Ilya," Hoare told the author, "and it was threatening to do something but never did. This opportunity came up with Kasabian and he was thinking, 'What shall I do? This is going to be full-on ...' and I basically think he felt, 'Well, I'm going to go for it and commit.' I think he recognised it might go somewhere whereas Ilya didn't. When Ian plays, the drums sound like an *instrument* rather than just a beat, if you know what I mean.[51] He just puts so much into it. As I played with him more, I realised he could turn his hand to pretty much any style, and you just know that he's gonna be reliable and rock-solid. I knew, if I'd book him for a gig, that it was going to be absolutely devastating. Mainly thanks in part to him, he was going to lift everyone just because of what he puts into it. The other thing about him I'd say is visually he's great to watch and that makes a difference. Any band with a drummer who's visually good to watch, people [enjoy] because it's just like the centre, it's driving the whole thing, and I think he's one of those people who, when he's playing, he commands attention."[52]

He even came into the organisation complete with his own nickname: 'Steak Daddy', which can only have helped matters. "One night in Bath about nine years ago," explains Dan Brown, also of Ilya, "Ian was sitting down to eat with a Bristol drum 'n' bass band called CCQ. They were due to play their set in about two hours, so most of the band decided to have a light snack. Not Ian though! Never one to give up the opportunity to chow down in style, he promptly ordered a *massive* steak dinner with all the trimmings. Everyone was impressed that he managed to get through the gig at all and the band were concerned that he may settle down for an after-dinner snooze at any moment. But in unparalleled style, he dealt with an hour and a half of high-octane drum-foolery with much aplomb, despite being internally sat on by half a cow. At the end of the gig, Bristol saxophone legend Craig Crofton introduced the band, and 'cause of the above, and also on account of the recent birth of Ian's eldest daughter, he shouted, 'Let's hear it for Steak Daddy on the drums!' The name stuck – although it has be shortened to 'Steak' or sometimes 'Steakio'. According to Ian, the name has got around with some fans – apparently a few years ago someone lobbed a Sainsburys sirloin onto the stage at a Kasabian gig!"

Meaty beats, a valid passport, plenty of experience and a sense of humour, it was always going to be a shoe-in that he would fit in with the Kasabian gang. Ian Matthews had finally solved that troublesome drummer spot in the band on a long-term basis.

As a debut album, *Kasabian* holds within it a kind of odd disparity of elements that somehow manage to blend the traditional songwriting process with mysticism, mystery and a dollop of revolution, too. This is, in part, because of the uniqueness of its birthing, of course, but also testament to the sonic meanderings and explorations engendered by lads messing about with vintage keyboards on the farm.

'Processed Beats' was recorded and subsequently tweaked more than once from its inception, of course. Ryan Glover remembers one particularly interesting session he was asked to contribute to during his time with the band.

"I remember when we were rehearsing in London, and they were tweaking some ideas for some songs with Jim Abbiss. Every now and then, they'd pop to the studio to see if he was finished, or to see what he'd done 'cause he was mixing or mastering at the time. I went down there and he phoned me up and said that he wanted me to take nothing but a pair of drumsticks and a snare drum down – and that was for 'Processed Beats'. I had to re-record just the snare drum. I was just sat there with about five or six mics round the snare drum, I was listening to the song and literally had one stick and the snare drum, and that's what I had to play along to. Whether they used it or not, I don't know, because the snare drum on 'Processed Beats' is quite apparent."

"I recorded 'Reason Is Treason' quite literally straight after a session we did for Zane Lowe for Radio One," recalls Glover the younger. "I was in the booth behind the glass, I think it was Serge and Chris Karloff chatting to Zane over the microphone, 'cause it was pre-recorded rather than live. That particular day, we had rehearsed and recorded four songs, basically live. I had about fifteen or twenty mics around my kit and the guys were spread around the room and played the live versions of the tracks. Which ones they used I don't know 'cause I'd left the band by then. I recorded 'Processed Beats', 'L.S.F.', 'Reason Is Treason' and 'Club Foot' for the session.

We went straight to the studio after the radio session – we were in London and I was expecting to go home, I had my kit packed and was knackered from playing the session so I was like, 'Ah, for Christ's sake!' But once I got in there I was okay, stayed the night in London and went home the next day. But basically we went straight there, to a studio in Mayfair. I got in there, the kit was set up and I was told to basically play along with the song, do whatever the hell I liked, do loads of fill-ins, drum fills, go crazy, 'Do what you want and we'll basically copy and paste and sample what we like and stick it down on the track.' That's what it was basically 'cause I was going nuts, making a few mistakes, stops and starts and going mental on the fill-ins so it wasn't completely live, but what you hear [on the record] is what I was playing, it was just cut and pasted, basically. It was [a right laugh].

A lot of people are surprised to hear that they put a tea towel over my snare drum to dampen it, although it comes out quite forceful. [Having the tea towel] was a bit weird at first but I got used to it after a while. You will not believe how many people have asked me what colour that tea towel was! It was blue and white squares – I put a hole through it after a while, that's how I remember – and the tea towel just went flying. That was good, I look back and I remember the tiredness I was feeling but I also look back on it with fondness 'cause I really enjoyed that session even though I was on the verge of collapsing. I think those guys stayed on and did more recording with the bass guitar and piano but I wasn't there for that. I just had to leave and get my head down in a hotel somewhere.

'Test Transmission' was done in the Hammersmith session. The kit was set up as usual, they placed a lot of emphasis, especially Serge, on my playing the drums as close as I could to how Ringo Starr or Charlie Watts would play it. They wanted me to play just consistent, the same volume and same level on the hi-hat. Obviously, when I play live, my natural style is to play the hi-hat with a lot of venom, but a lot of accenting, where not every hit is the same level or same hardness, but they said to me, 'We don't care how you play it but we want you to get that hi-hat really consistent.' And that is why the hi-hat, every single hit that you hear is consistent, the same level all the way through the song. I was there for ages doing this rhythm for them to sample, it's the most simple rock rhythm that a drummer can play. But that's just what they wanted – they wanted it to be simple but it was more about the feel and consistency of the rhythm that drove the song, and that's what they were trying to get and that's what I did.

A typical recording session, for the first few hours they'd work on different parts, playing different ways and stuff, different sections. I didn't actually play along to any drums at all, I never heard any drums in my earphones at all, only the click tracks as if I was playing live. Both recording sessions, I genuinely enjoyed. I loved hearing it back and I loved playing along, as tired as I was! It can get physically tiring, people don't realise how physically tiring it can be for a drummer playing for a couple of hours solid to a song. Especially 'Reason Is Treason', 'cause I was playing that over and over again until blood was coming out. But I look back on it with fondness, 'cause the results of all that hard work – the end result was amazing. I love those tracks, and I'm not just saying that 'cause I drummed on them. I liked those tracks beforehand. I was loving the whole album anyway, even before laying the drums down; I'm really thankful, being glad to have been a part of it in general."

The results speak for themselves.

Listening to *Kasabian*, it is hugely coherent, some feat by all concerned to pull often incredibly disparate tunes and sonics together over a disjointed and often frustrating year or so.

"The first two or three tunes I did," reveals producer Jim Abbiss, "were mostly the singles and were 90% done, there might've been one little overdub to do, or a backing vocal or something, but pretty much a mix, that was it. As time progressed, I got sent more and more stuff at different stages because the band and the label were looking for someone who would be kinda honest and say, 'That's fine, leave it alone' and, 'This one actually needs quite a bit more work and [to] tie it all together.'

A bone of contention, I think, for the press side of Kasabian [was that] although they like some of the [obviously referenced] things that they've latched onto, there's so much stuff that never gets mentioned that's influenced them. Obviously they're massive fans of a great deal of Sixties psychedelia and a great deal of Seventies prog rock and experimental music and Krautrock and various other things, but those sort of things are never picked up on, it's all like, 'Oh, they must like the Stone Roses' or something. Well, yeah, they probably do, but they don't write songs because of that! They're into Tangerine Dream, Can, Kraftwerk, The Stones, The Beatles, The Who and odder things from the Sixties, Silver Apples and more experimental kinda psychedelic folk things – all very important bands to them. I'd have to really stop and think to remember half the stuff that we'd talked about, but it was certainly not the Madchester scene."

"We've all stayed friends right up to this day," beams Barny. "So it's just a bit of luck that both me, Jim and all the band got on really well and saw eye to eye musically. Working with them was always a bit like mucking around with your mates, to be honest. It's not like a job, it's how music should be really. 90% of the time it isn't! It's very lucky we all kind of paired up [as collaborators on the project] and hit it off. It always seems like fun and not hard work, which is a good thing."

There are also several references to tunes and melodies that had been in the band's minds for a number of years, albeit recontexted and revamped on occasion. One of the most clear of these is 'I.D.', which brings a beaty, groovy, cinematic framework around the format of the Saracuse track, 'Lost Soul', which in its acoustic form held within it the fragile power and belief that has survived nearly intact to its *Kasabian* incarnation. The 'Lost Soul' concept helped name the single 'L.S.F. (Lost Souls Forever)' although it had become known as 'L.S.F.' through a misprint on a particular demo, its initial title having been 'Good Souls Forever' or 'G.S.F.' – the G being mistaken for an L by the record company ... and a new title is born. It also shares a rather interesting coincidental musical counterpart, with the introduction and the chorus of the Beach Boys' 'Kokomo' having a similar rhythmical aesthetic sensibility. 'Club Foot' also appears to utilise some of the same samples as Saracuse's 'Come Back Down', particularly the bell-type sounds toward the end of the track. 'Test Transmission', meanwhile, nods at the ultimately unsuccessful 'Rain', using that same vocal melody in a new and very satisfying way with very different lyrics. The backward guitars and samples here serve to reinforce the psychedelic edge that the farm had added to the already adept songwriting that had long been the group's aim and delight.

From the extremely accessible singles to the sonic sketches, and despite (or perhaps, because of) the various drummers and approaches, the album sounded like absolutely nothing else that was around at the time, or since, for that matter. Full marks all round.

"I think he was responsible for that LP beginning to sound like it ended up sounding," opines Nick Raymonde. "It was pretty much formed by the band and Jacknife Lee on that farm, and what was done afterwards was to make it sound sonically accessible. It was Jacknife who got what it was that they were trying to do, and in a sense taught them how to apply those sounds within the group in a way that wouldn't make them sound like producer add-ons but make them sound like things that they would actually be able to play, which is how they sound now when you see them live."

"Jim came in and got the job done," concludes Jacknife by way of fair balance. "Also at the time I worked on the music by myself at home and this was a mistake because the band felt excluded and we stopped seeing eye to eye. The final versions and my versions are not that dissimilar, to be honest it sounds similar to the album, [but] the final recording is bigger and fatter. One of the reasons why my work wasn't used, I guess, was my methods of storing, filing, and usage of audio was not very typical (or professional, it was my first record). I would bounce the whole string recording down to stereo files to process, same with drums, so going back generations to find the original takes was difficult and pointless as I would have altered it so much it was quicker to redo it all. [With] time and increased confidence, the band got better over the months we worked together and Jim is great. I think the process with Jim was a more enjoyable one for them."

"It's a very cocky album," Serge pointed out, "because it's a debut album and it's quite epic you know, and Tom, when he sings, he doesn't give a fuck what anyone thinks about him, you know? He's *him*, and that's the beauty … There's not a band for the masses any more. There's nothing wrong in appealing to the masses as long as you're trying stuff new. Cause essentially it's just connecting with people."

"A lot of the tunes, they mean a lot to he and you and her and whatever," he said a little mystifyingly, pointing his finger at random people. "But I'm not going to tell them what they mean to *me*, that's something which you can decide yourself. But they're pretty much thoughts from everyday life. The past few years have been mental for everyone, they're kind of talking about that in some shape or form. Whether it's love or fighting, or drugs or sex, you know. I think it's a very psychedelic album."

Tom, as usual, had something to add to the mix. "We're just a band that likes grooving and moving and going for it," he said. "And there's still the rock elements to it, it's still there, they're all there. You put 'Reason Is Treason' on, and that'll kick the fuck out of anything that's in its way. That's my opinion on it, you know. But it's all there, man, it's all there. We just hope people are grateful!"

CHAPTER FOURTEEN

Nuts

The album went into the UK charts at Number 4 on September 12, an impressive feat for a group who were, a mere year before, playing to crowds of two hundred people on the toilet circuit. The band had also played a triumphant homecoming gig the previous night, Serge and the boys returning to DeMontford Hall after the disappointment of the *Red Leicester* non-appearance all those years ago. The album's great reception was boosted even further when *Q* Magazine nominated Kasabian as 'Best New Band' alongside the likes of Keane, Franz Ferdinand, Razorlight, Maroon 5, The Killers, The Zutons and Snow Patrol. With the group beginning to seriously pull in the coverage, they appeared on the front of several magazines during September, 2004, including *The Big Issue*, where they talked about their triumphant appearance at the Japanese festival, Summersonic, the previous month.

The band were also anxious to reaffirm their Leicester credentials and the fact that, contrary to some of their contemporaries, they were lads firmly with their feet on the ground. "It's quite a comforting thing to have, you know, your football team," pondered Serge. "You know your dad took you when you were a kid and it always reminds you of being close. Football became very fashionable at one point and then it became very unfashionable. But it's not about that at all. It's like, we support Leicester and that's that. It's good, 'cause when you go down, you meet all your old friends and shit, and it's good to have that. They're the ones that take the piss out of you for wearing a stupid hat. You need that. Like, what's all this bullshit about? They'll go, 'What the fuck is that jacket!?'"

Still, anyone could have been forgiven for having their heads slightly turned: at this stage the gigs were beset by hoardes of journalists, as well as the huge amount of Kasabian fans excited by the release of the album. Pete Oag was a member of Trap 2, support band for several dates.

"The Scala in Kings Cross on the first tour [we did with them] was in the week that the Kasabian record was released," he told me. "And there was a massive buzz around the place. It was pretty fucking surreal, crawling with Japanese journalists in the backstage area. The band were getting presented with some kind of gold record-type manoeuvre for selling a hundred thousand records in a week. For a band like us at the time, to see that kind of thing was pretty inspiring and it was one of the best experiences of my life. It was very surreal, probably for them too, not just us."

There was just time to re-release 'Processed Beats' (the single getting to Number 17 on October 11, 2004), complete with video that involved being, "in the woods somewhere. I think it's where they shot *Gladiator*," according to Serge. "Basically, we're just on acid in the woods, I think."

"My prevailing memory for the whole tour was the live experience," continues Oag, who now plays in the band Little Ze. "They opened every gig we supported them on with 'I.D.', and it was a song that perfectly summed them up at the time, that massive intro then that triumphant moment when it all kicks in, Tom strides onto the stage and the lights kick in. It used to send shivers up my spine every night. It was obvious we were a part of something massive, something very special, a part of history, if you like, it's forever etched into my memory. I remember feeling really embraced by them, we spent time with them before and after each gig, wishing them luck literally as they were going onstage and that. They're just real people, no real egos despite the circus of attention that was surrounding them. There was a gig at Leeds Blank Canvas which, at the time, was probably the biggest headline gig they'd done, and it was like an aircraft hangar. The place was buzzing and there were loads of Japanese youngsters camped out in front of the stage three or four hours before the gig, *NME* journalists backstage, it was very surreal for us again."

There was also a rare opportunity to take it all in, Pete says: "I remember being stood at the back of the venue with Tom, about midnight, after the place had cleared out, just stood with him marvelling at the sheer enormity of the whole thing, really. The geezer was on cloud nine, wading through loads of empty pint pots in the hall, just thinking about what had happened. It was special to be part of it, to see how far they'd come."

Thoughtful times aside, of course, this being Kasabian there was always room for some bonhomie, and the Trap 2 guys were more than happy to help out when needed. "There was basically a big drink-up most nights. The Liquidroom in Edinburgh was, I think, the last gig of the second tour. They'd have everyone into their dressing room afterwards, both support bands, all their management team and that, then more often than not go back to the tourbus and have a game of PlayStation and ... whatever. That night was unbelievable. They were just as popular, if not more popular, north of the border. It was about one thirty in the morning, we went to go back to the tour bus and basically Tom and Serge were accosted by a group of six or seven of the most obsessive Scottish girls I'd ever seen in my life! They'd been waiting in the freezing cold for hours and Tom's trying to fend them off, tossing me his mobile phone which has got the code for the bus in it, 'Quick, get the code out!' Upstairs, ten minutes later, you could still hear them pounding on the bus outside and [someone shouted], 'Go downstairs, tell any one of them you're in Kasabian and she'll nosh you off!' But I didn't bother. I just carried on playing PlayStation to be honest with you!" No doubt the girls in question were just after a quick game of *Scrabulous*, of course, but it certainly brings home the point that Kasabian were now Bona Fide Rock Stars.

The group returned to Japan for a series of gigs that November, keeping the releases flowing with a tour-specific EP, as well as something a little more curious, and certainly very cool. Mark Vidler of Go Home Productions created a fascinating take on 'Processed Beats', which he spliced with the Stone Roses' track, 'Waterfall', to produce the aptly-named 'Processed Waterfall', which subsequently became a huge hit on white label in the clubs. This kind of support was absolutely vital to Kasabian, whose radio support was just starting to kick in but they weren't quite yet ubiquitous.

"I knew of Kasabian by then, I was a big fan of theirs. And they said, 'The band are really big fans of Public Enemy, Stone Roses,

Primal Scream, try mixing it with things like that,' so 'Waterfall' came to mind and that was how it basically came about. I tried a few things with Public Enemy and it wasn't really sitting well. I tried 'Waterfall' out, and it fitted like a dream. 'Processed Waterfall' really took off. It was quite big.

I like to think it helped them get them a play in certain clubs that they probably wouldn't have got played in at the time. I did it tastefully. There are some times when artists ask you to put them with someone you just wouldn't think of putting them with but with this particular track it actually blended really well."[53]

'Butcher Blues', from the Islington Academy gig, was also made available for download through iTunes, the proceeds going toward the charity, War Child. Once back from Japan, the group set about recording a video for 'Cutt Off', also to be re-released imminently, with respected director Simon Willows, featuring Tom striding through a cityscape full of all the characters, weirdos and wasters you'd expect. It brings to mind, slightly, the famous video for 'Bittersweet Symphony' by The Verve in atmosphere although the music is, of course, widely different.

The band nipped over to New York to debut at the Bowery Ballroom on November 19, a gig that was enthused about by the American press and the relatively small crowd present. An early shot across the bows from the Leicester possee, and another statement of intent. Kasabian embarked on another tour of the Barfly venues, for the MTV 'Gonzo On Tour' gigs that also featured, amongst others, The Go! Team and Hot Chip. And though the venues were smallish, the vibe was inevitably massive. The year came to an end in some triumph, with the group snagging their debut *NME* cover.

"We have been waiting seven years for it, mate," enthused a beaming Tom. "When it happens to you, you can't believe it. They had to put us on there. There was nothing they could do about it. They had to write about us. It's a wonderful thing. I remember buying an *NME* when I was sixteen-years-old. Richard Ashcroft was on the cover. I was thinking to myself, *Wouldn't it be amazing one day if they put us on there?* We got on there. We were laughing at the picture. We felt like kids again. It's a proud moment."[54]

On December 16, Serge's birthday, another proud moment came at Brixton Academy for a gig that was recorded in high quality (and later released as a download-only album) – and followed by a huge post-gig celebration. It had been a phenomenal year for Kasabian:

they had convinced the UK that they were, indeed, the new force in music. The album was finally out and about, the gigs were coming thick and fast. It was time to take it out into the big, wide world.

EMPIRE

CHAPTER FIFTEEN

Bringing Civilization
To The World

2005 would begin with the re-release of 'Cutt Off', the first widespread official release of a record that had only previously been circulated to the tune of a thousand copies. Interestingly, one of the B-sides was a remix by American counterparts Mad Action, friends of the band (and soon to play rather a larger part in the story). The CD2 version of 'Cutt Off' that was later put out by the record label also featured the video as well as versions of 'Processed Beats' and the dub classic 'Out Of Space', which was famously cut up and sampled by The Prodigy. Those latter two tracks were taken from the band's Radio One 'Live Lounge' session, and had previously been unavailable. As ever with Kasabian, there was plenty of musical material to choose from, and with the fans eager to get their hands on every scrap and snippet of audio possible, the single crashed into the UK charts at a very impressive Number 8.

The Movement was as fervent as ever, although by this stage the concept of underground heroes seeking to overthrow the mainstream was beginning to become a little obsolete. The Movement may have been a special force, with a nucleus of a few hundred, but the band had truly cracked it in the UK and sign-ups to The Movement on the band's website (which had won a BT Digital Music Award the previous year) were becoming enormous.

"The Movement couldn't really sustain a huge amount of people," says Amanda McGowan. "It was good for what it was used as initially, which was basically getting the word about, but once people had started getting into it there wasn't really a need for it anymore and it slowly disbanded. We really loved the band and thought they deserved to be mainstream and we would do anything to help them get there. I still talk to a few people now and again who used to run around and stencil stuff and run away, but we kind of stopped talking to each other after a while. A lot of The Movement crossed over to Chikinki." Still, with Kasabian's music becoming more mainstream, the Movement could always switch on the likes of *Desperate Housewives* or *CSI Miami* to get their fix of the Leicester lads …

There was talk that Serge was up for a part in a movie adaptation of the life of Marie Antoinette (although probably not the title part), supposedly to be directed by Sofia Coppola. Perhaps it was the Italian link that did it, but it came to nothing and remained just newspaper talk. Testament, if nothing else, to the growing stature and general coolness of Kasabian that they were even being talked about in such circles.

Their stature was confirmed with the release on January 11 of the Brit Awards nominations for that year. Kasabian were up in no less than three categories: 'Best British Group' (along with Franz Ferdinand, Keane, Muse and Snow Patrol), 'Best British Rock Act' (other nominees being The Libertines, Franz Ferdinand, Keane, Muse and Snow Patrol, and the winner to be chosen by readers of rock mag *Kerrang!*), and 'Best British Live Act', where their counterparts were Franz Ferdinand, Muse, The Libertines and Steak's mate, Jamie Cullum. For a band to be nominated at all for even one of these high profile awards on the back of an admittedly stunning debut album was astonishing, but to be in with a shout of no less than three awards was absolutely incredible. On January 31, the *Brit 25* album was released in conjunction with the announcement, featuring both the single and video of 'L.S.F. (Lost Souls Forever)'. Kasabian then recorded a full live set at Maida Vale Studios on January 13 before an invited audience for BBC Radio One, which was subsequently broadcast on Steve Lamacq's show on February 7. Tom Meighan had picked up a chest infection, however, leading to the cancellation of dates at Heidelberg on January 31 and the following night's Berlin show, but he would have been cheered up on February 1 when *NME* announced that Kasabian were nominated for 'Best Band' and 'Best New Band' in their own forthcoming awards. Recognition was coming thick and fast, and the singer recovered enough to join the band again as they first ripped it up in Tokyo then Osaka on February 5 and 6, with the headliners for those two Japanese dates being the American rockers Good Charlotte.

"We were there for like four days," explained Chris Dibs. "We just reached Japan and hung out the weekend and then came back. We were the first non-Japanese band to play on Tower Records, which was pretty cool, on top of Tower Records and [this] gig for competition winners and fans."[(55)]

The band were in the grip of an inexorable whirlwind of activity, although they were ultimately to be disappointed to not pick up any of the Brit Awards for which they had been nominated. "I bumped into Tom at their first Brit Awards," says journalist Kim Dawson of the *Daily Star*, "And he was not impressed they hadn't won. But rather than diss anyone he seemed more energised about coming back stronger next time. They went from newcomers to British Rock nominees. Not bad! Half Kasabian's appeal is that they speak the truth. The fans know they are buying into something real – a bunch of blokes they could consider mates. Tom is a dream interviewee – one of my all-time favourites. Serge is more reserved, but equally doesn't hold back an opinion. Every journo wants a strong headline and vibrant copy. With loads of manufactured pop acts media-trained to death, Kasabian was a welcome release. They are down-to-earth honest lads and they've got every right to diss someone if they don't like them. Kasabian are a band of the people who simply have the balls to say what many of their indie schmindie counterparts are too scared of, in case it affects their sales."

No rest for the wicked, and despite the disappointment of not picking up the Brit gongs this time around, the boys played the *NME* show to celebrate that particular award nomination on February 10.

Keeping up the inventive side of matters, it was also announced that 'L.S.F. (Lost Souls Forever)' would be one of the tracks used in a project with national charity Youth Music, music community site dBass, Apple's Garageband software and the *Times Educational Supplement*. Essentially, the separate parts of the track, such as bass, guitar, drums, vocals etc, would be all made available for download by those who signed up to the project for that charity. Subsequently, the remixes created would be entered into a competition over various age groups, with prizes including gadgets and widgets from Apple and others. Anyone, therefore, could step into the shoes of the likes of Jagz and Jacknife for a day. Incredible to think that this was technically possible, and the fact that Kasabian were so ready to become involved in this project is partly down to the way that they discovered their own muse through cheapish PC software down the years..

There is one place, however, that a band must always look to when attempting to conquer the world, in building an empire for their continued worldwide success and domination, and that is the United States of America. Kasabian had long-since fulfilled their prophecies of turning the British music scene on its head, but any band in it for the long haul has to look across the pond for the next stage of their career. That Kasabian chose to do this so frighteningly early on is down to their work ethic and fearless belief that anything was, indeed, possible. The plan was to hit most of the major US (and Canadian) cities during February and March 2005, in conjunction with similarly-rising UK act The Music, a band from Leeds whose affection with the breakbeat and the dancy side of indie rock made them a very hot proposition at the time. The tour would also take in the influential SXSW (South By Southwest) and Coachella events. As ever, Kasabian were on the interview trail, chatting to anyone and everyone who requested a few minutes of their time, letting all and sundry know what to expect from the gigs.

"We have half an hour to blow them away," said Chris Dibs. "It's a bit shorter set than we're used to but we've lined up seven cracking songs and it's a bit more rockin'. A bit more rock 'n' roll than the album. It's a lot more live vicious sounds. It's going to blow people away."[56] Meighan was in good form too, promising that the band was, "Going to be on fire. We are going to be locked and loaded. We are going to be ready to go. We are going to give you our heart and our blood, man. We are going to give you a rock 'n' roll show. We are going to spill our blood. We are not lying to you. You are going to fucking believe it. It's going to be like an electric pole fucking hitting you really hard in the balls. It's going to throw you around. You are going to love it."[57]

Vintage stuff. The gigs were, almost without exception, as good as the singer had promised, the Leicester boys hammering out the modern classics and knocking people's heads off with their sounds left, right and centre as they blazed a trail across the States.[58]

"I saw first-hand that half of the crowd walked out of the 9:30 Club after Kasabian left the stage, myself included," wrote influential blogger Elizabeth of Music Capitol concerning the band's gig in Washington, D.C. on February 18. "Not only did much of the crowd come just to see Kasabian, the band put on such a loud, energetic, and epic performance that these concert goers were satisfied for the evening." Kasabian, it appeared, were doing on this tour what they had previously done on the Cooper Temple Clause and Chikinki tours, and that is to subsume the tour fans into Kasabian fans.

When back in the UK, the band were not dragging their feet as far as new material was concerned, either, with Serge putting down ideas on his own set-up wherever he could. As the bandwagon rolled back to Britain, studio sessions were set up wherever possible.

"I was doing B-sides and stuff," says Simon Barnicott, "that they would just knock up as a bit of fun, as a B-side should be, and a few demos and stuff. They were started off by Serge at his place and again we just finished off when we were mixing and stuff."

Despite the album still providing singles (both 'Cutt Off' and 'Club Foot' were re-released on April 17 on different formats, reaching Number 192 and 59 in the charts respectively) there were, even at a very early stage (going back to 2004, even), songs being mooted for the follow-up to *Kasabian*.

"They played me [a song called] 'Empire' just after we finished the first record," continues Barny. "When we started doing the B-sides. They played me that and it was good. Serge is always writing tons of stuff and zillions of ideas. I heard it *very* early on."

April 2005 saw Kasabian return for a series of UK dates, although the first night of the tour at Glasgow's Academy, April 22, was cut short after Serge had been caught square on the bonce by a stray flying bottle. It had come three quarters of the way through the band's set but Pizzorno was forced to head to a nearby hospital for six stitches.

"I was told by a doctor not to continue the show," he explained in a press release. "It's such a shame the actions of one person put an end to our best gig all year. I would like to thank the Glasgow fans for their support and look forward to seeing them tonight. Please throw bras and knickers from now on."

As the summer started knocking, there was just time for the group to hit the Radio One Big Weekend in Sunderland, May 5 2005, alongside the likes of Foo Fighters, Natalie Imbruglia and Chemical

Brothers, before it was time for the group to build on the good will and fanbase they'd begun to accumulate in America once more, returning for fifteen dates alongside Mad Action.

"We had the same manager so that was how we met each other," revealed that band's Ryan Bernstein when I asked him about those days. "When I first met them they were this band he was working with, I didn't really know much about this music or anything. We were in the UK, my bandmate Paul and I, and we would just end up hanging out with these guys 'cause we all really got along. Then the record came out and greatness was shed upon them. From that point on, they got their tours lined up, they asked us to go on tour with them on two or three occasions and we did forty or fifty shows together.[59]

We were on tour with them as the transition was occurring for them, when they went from some band that nobody had ever heard of and then you knew something was gonna go beyond for them. You could kinda smell that their next tour was gonna be bigger, then the next one was gonna be bigger.

Before shows they were always doing interviews and getting their photos taken and you could tell that people were interested outside of, of course, the fans. Cause the shows were always all sold out or very close. You just kinda get that sense, 'cause we're hanging around all day before the show and walking around saying, 'What the hell are we gonna do [to fill in time]? And Tom and Serge would typically be pretty damned busy with interviews and this and that. You could tell that the powers behind them were kinda happening for them. The fans believed in them and also the people they were working with, you can see it, you can tell."

During the May tour, however, the band were still plugging away to turn people's heads: this was, indeed, a mission they were on, and there was no doubt whatsoever that they were up for the challenge, even if the crowds were a little more tricky to turn on at times.

"The UK response is just more enthusiastic about them," muses Ryan Bernstein. "The crowd goes insane whereas American crowds don't do that so much; they don't let you know in the same way that a UK crowd who's behind a band from their hometown [would]. It's a different response, same idea in a sense – they're obviously far bigger in the UK than in America but same response, lots of people at the shows but they're like superstars in the UK. It's different here for them. Most people probably don't know who they are here [yet]."

Serge himself was enjoying himself, despite the occasional small crowd. "It's good for the soul, man," he told an interviewer in Toronto. "You get used to playing these big venues and expect it. We started in the clubs. We can play in front of fifty or five million and it's exactly the same. It's the spirit of the band, man. We're having a great time in America, just trying to stay alive."[60] This echoed Tom's sentiments immediately post-Glasto the previous year, when he had told an interviewer that the band hadn't, "had any substances. We got here this morning, played, and now we just want to wade about and take it all in. We'll chill later, keeping to our motto which is simply to 'stay alive.'"[61] Meanwhile, Chris Karloff was literally continuing the love affair with America, meeting a New York lass during this period who turned his worldview upside down.

Then it was time to revisit the scene of one of many of 2004's triumphs, as the band stepped back onstage for the summer festivals in the UK. First up was an appearance at Glastonbury, on June 25. A storming performance on the Other Stage included a new song, 'Stuntman', one of the first fruits of their growing new set of tracks as they began to look toward the future. It was nothing less than triumphant. The band then went on to wow crowds at Oxegyn, Belfast on July 9 (where they played an impromptu acoustic set for fifty people in the VIP tent as well as ripping it up on the second stage), then T In The Park the very next day.

Living arrangements had also altered by now: the farm's huge strength had always been that it was a base, an escape to allow the group to scheme and plan musical and career matters. However, since the release of *Kasabian*, the boys had been out on tour virtually constantly, and when they were back at home, it was for a matter of days at a time rather than weeks in which to stretch out and explore. Sure, songs were being written, but Serge always had been very prolific. However, the farm had outlived its usefulness as a base from which to direct operations, and the chaps moved, variously, to London and then eventually back to Leicester itself, although Karloff spent his time in New York as much as was practical.

2005 kept bringing the good stuff: the band returned to Japan for Summersonic 2005, before they fulfilled a long-standing ambition – touring with Oasis. The gigs, which also featured Aussie rockers Jet, spanned September 2005 and brought the band even closer to Noel and Liam, who had long been shouting from the rooftops about the spiritual successors to their crown.

Meighan, as a huge fan of Star Wars, was even interviewed for the movie's official website; his propensity for wearing his Darth Vader T-shirt onstage had not gone unnoticed. In the interview he named *Revenge Of The Sith* as his favourite film in the series, and since having seen it during the summer, he'd grown a beard, rumour had it in order to look as much like Obi-Wan Kenobi as was possible.[62]

Back on Earth, there were also whispers that Kasabian would even work with Noel on some new material at his home studio. "We're talking about doing some stuff with them, but I don't know that anything will come of that," Gallagher said. "They are more than welcome in my studio, and there's a chance I might be doing some songs. I hope it does [happen] – it will be great."[63]

The gigs, once more, were amazing, and by the time their stint opening for Oasis was over, Tom Meighan explained about how big a deal it really had been for Kasabian. "We've had some great gigs, and some good nights. It's just been an amazing time for us." Not least appearing onstage with Oasis for a cover of 'My Generation', knocking down two influences with one jubilant stone. There had also been a fair amount of offstage hi-jinks on the month long tour, Meighan said.

"It's a brotherhood!" he noted. "'Soul brothers' is what Noel says. [Liam] is as mad as a hatter! Fucking nuts. But I understand exactly where he's coming from. I feel his vibe; I feel Noel's vibe. We're buzzing. Serge and Liam were going on a mad one, diving in the swimming pool fully clothed, fucking going nuts."[64]

Gallagher the elder also revealed an interesting technique that the Kasabian camp had for calming down the ever-energetic Meighan – take him to a toyshop for half an hour to mess about with the newest remote control robots and cars. Noel had experienced it first hand when Meighan, on top form, had invaded the Oasis dressing room.

"Somebody turned up," laughed the mono-browed songwriting hero, "And put him in a cab to take him to Toys 'R' Us in Times Square, calm him down, because of all the flashing lights and he plays with the toys and then he's alright. That's fucking genius, man!"[65]

There was just time for the self-proclaimed 'Leicester's Greatest Export Since Engelbert Humperdinck' to head over to Monaco, no less, for the annual *Fashion Rocks* event: pairing up with Burberry, the band lent their growing presence to the event which serves as a fundraiser for the Prince's Trust charity, with the band playing 'Processed Beats' as a succession of gorgeous women modelled Christopher Bailey's designs for that label.

It had been an amazing time on the road, for sure, and the band were absolutely on fire about the new material they'd been writing; whether recordings were to take place with Noel or not, it was an old collaborator to whom they were to turn.

CHAPTER SIXTEEN

Red Card

"I had kept in contact with the band," producer Jim Abbiss recalls of the latter days of 2005. "I'd hoped to do more with them because we got on so well, but I never expect for that to happen with anyone I work with. These days, a career can be short and if you get the chance to work with different people that excite you, then you should have a go at doing that. I hoped to do more with Kasabian, we sort of talked towards the end of the live and I talked to Serge quite a bit. Then I got a call from the label saying, 'We'd like to put you on hold for a few months at the end of the year to do some work on the second record,' so I was really pleased."

This would prove to be an interesting project for all concerned. The debut album had been conceived in an utterly unique situation, with the group living together on that farm in the middle of nowhere, with access to lots of time, lots of records, and odds and sods of occasionally dodgy audio gear, almost recording in secret and with a very low profile. Now, however, the Kasabian boys were sitting on top of an album approaching sales near the one million mark, had been to Japan and America, and were hanging out with megastars of music, plus appearing on *Soccer AM, CD:UK* and even taking part in penalty shoot outs at half-time in Leicester City matches! Clearly, there was a need to think about the best way to create an environment in which to allow the creative juices to flow away from such a spotlight. This time around, however, the big advantage was precisely that there *was* a finite time in which to get the project nailed.

"This is the inevitable thing that happens with the majority of bands," ponders Abbiss. "That they have the whole lifetime to demo and write their first album and then they have three months to do the whole thing on the second, if that. They no longer had their base at the farm so they were living out of hotel rooms half the time and demo-ing on a laptop on a tour-bus. I thought it would be quite important to not make it a formal kind of recording, where we started on a Monday and [had] a timetable of things and you finish at *this time* and that's it. Some people and some albums are very tight and formalised, so I thought it was important to go somewhere they could relax and have their own sort of demo space – a little bit like the farm, or as near to it as we could get, but we'd also have a bigger studio sitting there when they were ready. Then when it was right, we'd go in and record stuff and they could take it away on their own [to work on it more] if they wanted to or we could all work on it together."

The ideal place for that kind of approach is a residential studio, in this case the legendary Rockfield in south Wales, where everyone from Motörhead to Led Zep and the Stone Roses had previously laid tracks down to tape. "It started off pretty much with all Serge's demos, like the first one," says Barny, engineer on the sessions. "But they weren't anywhere near as finished. At that point, they'd played a lot more live and became a lot more of a band. Everything started from Serge's demos ... but I think the whole point was to make it a bit more of a band-based project because they were a bit more [of a tighter unit than the first album] as they'd been playing live [loads]."

Though the plans were sound, a bombshell was about to be dropped that would impact hugely not only on the final album, but on Kasabian as a whole. This was a gang of mates who had been together, effectively, for around ten years: Tom, Serge, Dibs and Karloff were always the nucleus from which everything else would emanate, and those strong friendships had been intensified by the experiences over the course of the journey from 'Shine On' to Summersonic festivals, from early gigs at The Viper Club to jumping into American swimming pools in the middle of the night with a cackling Liam Gallagher. The group had become part of each other's musical DNA at the farm in Rutland, they'd seen America, witnessed a wider world at work, and were well on the way to grasping a part of it for themselves.

Or were they?

Since the farm posse had split up, Chris Karloff had become hugely enamoured with life in New York, and had married his long-term girlfriend over there in November 2005; subsequently the guitarist decided to live there and drink in the famous city's excitement and history. This was great for the ever-explorative mind of the boy Pratt, but in terms of his status as part of the gang that had met in parks in Blaby to shout and dream, it was a seismic shift. Returning to the UK for the new album sessions was naturally not so convenient anymore, and so it was mooted that the band might consider recording at a studio nearer his new base in The Big Apple, an idea which, perhaps understandably, got short shrift.

"They've known each other for a long time," notes Jim Abbiss. "They went to schools together and to suddenly have someone who didn't want to record in England, [couldn't] go to any of the party things they would normally have done together, it was kinda hard, I think, for them to relate to him in the same way."

Although Karloff and Serge had written a few tracks together over the course of the touring of 2004 and 2005, there were also a few musical clashes brewing between the pair as to what direction the new album was to take: Karloff's love for the cinematic and electronic married to Serge's love for the psychedelic, Big Rock sonics were in part what had made *Kasabian* such an interesting album, but this time around, the disparate elements were causing a little more creative friction between the pair. This sort of subjective conflict was not uncommon in a creative unit, nor was it an insurmountable problem, according to their producer.

"Serge very much starts ideas off, so he's the main focus of the writing process, and on the first album, there'd be, from what I can gather, a lot of sparring off Chris Karloff, and there was less of that on the second record .... Karloff was still involved on the second record in the writing process but not so involved at all in the recording process ... I think [there was more to it than] the disagreements over some things musically, which I don't think were that massive.

Chris just completely changed his lifestyle over the space of two years, and went from being very much one of the gang, to very much a distant person with his new girlfriend and wife ... I think they suddenly found themselves trying to write with someone that they weren't hanging out with [daily]."

For a band based round the 'gang' concept, a group whose whole raison d'etre had been based on the ultra-strong relationships between themselves, this was an unfortunate development. To be fair to both sides, Chris had just fallen in love with an American and the band had just wanted to continue a creative process that had ben so fruitful to date. It was merely an unfortunate development, but not one that either party could control.

"Chris and Serge were both leaders," muses the *Daily Star*'s Kim Dawson. "And, in the end, Serge's friendship with Tom put them naturally at the forefront. Most people won't realise Chris did a huge chunk of creating the first album with Serge. The second record was very different ... they took a risk. It was a shock when he left."

A shock to everybody, not least the personalities who had spent a long time with, and even in, the band, including one of their former drummers. "I never saw it [coming]," says Ryan Glover. "Never in a million years [did I expect him to leave]. When I saw the nucleus of Kasabian I thought, 'Fair enough, it could be me and possibly a few other drummers in the future, like Oasis have gone through a few drummers. That's okay,' but I'd never envision any of them leaving. Because they all thought on the same wavelength. Chris was obviously part of the songwriting team as well and I never actually envisioned him leaving. I basically thought those guys would be together throughout their career."

As 'the quiet one', says Amanda McGowan, who spent a lot of time with the band as one of the founder members of The Movement, "Chris used to sit in the background. I think it got to a point where he wasn't happy with what was going on."

The truth is that a combination of more complex factors was, indeed, at work in Karloff and the rest of the band deciding to go their separate ways. "Jim told me Chris was just fed up," says Ben Cole, a good friend of the Pratt family. "He always seemed to be like the lad who wanted to settle down. It seemed to be important to him, and though it sounds a bit sappy, I think that's definitely what he wanted to do. He found his girl in New York and moved over there so I think that he was on a different trajectory to the rest of them, whether that's musically or what he wanted to do with the rest of his life."

"I'm not sure if [touring] is the thing he wanted to miss out on. He's still pursuing music, and doing some stuff with the guy who used to be in The Shining. I think it was the lifestyle thing and definitely the music as well ..."

Nick Raymonde feels that the eventual departure of the erstwhile guitarist and fan of the esoteric side of matters had a massive impact on the group as a whole.

"The thing that must have changed it quite dramatically was Chris Karloff leaving the band, because he really was a big influence," he says. "And if there is some metaphysical, transcendental element in their music, I think a large amount of that came from him because I think he was a very spiritual kind of person. Not that I had any conversations with him that would lead me to make that conclusion, he's probably more concerned with other things than he is with anything of that level or maybe he's [now] a Buddhist monk! He could be, but then so could Tom because that's what their appeal was. In a sense, you never wanted to dig too deep into what they were really like as blokes and individuals because in a sense you would shatter the glass. There was a real pleasure being with them and that was a lot of fun. It's always the best fun when you sign a band and you get that sense of thinking it's just *great fun* being with them. And that's what they were like; you'd come back from a trip with them with just loads of stories for days and days about things they'd got up to, things they'd said, stuff like that."

And Chris Karloff had been a huge part of that. But then again, even before he'd joined up with Serge, Tom and Dibs, they comprised the initial core of the group; they had, in a sense, only to get back to their roots to find the answer within themselves, albeit that it took an event of such magnitude to stimulate them into action once more. After all, they'd managed to shrug off the loss of several drummers over the years and still stood tall at the cutting edge of music. Would this be any different?

"There was probably a week or so of people not really knowing where they stood," observes Barny Barnicott. "And being a bit frustrated with everything, and I think by the end of it everyone really just wanted to know [what was going to happen next].

It's just how they changed – from being Serge and Chris in their bedroom to actually touring and gigging, and becoming a bit more of a live thing. I think obviously Serge was into different sorts of music as well, and the stuff he was into was more live kind of things [than Chris]. Psychedelic stuff and not so drum machiney-proggy kind of stuff … I think all of us, me and Jim included, would have loved for Pratty to be about and be a part of it but there came a point towards the end where we all just realised that it's not gonna happen like that, and it's not like we didn't have anything good done, so we just thought, 'Well, let's just get on with it.' It was very different for me and Jim 'cause we didn't have that sort of relationship that Serge and Chris had so it wasn't too difficult for us. But tricky for them. It ended up, on the second record, to be honest, that Serge had to step forward and say, 'Right, I'm doing [it] and it took him a little while to get his head round that, but he did it brilliantly."

And so, unbeknownst to the rest of the world, Kasabian had become a four-piece, even whilst they were recording the follow-up to the ultra-successful first album. Such mysteries are kept under wraps rather easier in the middle of nowhere and if there was ever a set of people with the personality and self-belief to see them over a such a debilitating bump in their path, it was these boys.

CHAPTER SEVENTEEN

Empire Building

With Serge now firmly ensconced as main writer, and the uncertainty over Karloff's status in the band at last resolved, the sessions at Rockfield could finally begin in earnest.

"There's pressure from everybody [with a second album]," says Jim Abbiss, "because suddenly there's obviously a lot more riding on it, there's a lot more people whose jobs are riding on this group of people who are trying to write their tunes without thinking about any of that. But I tried to keep any pressure that was coming in from outside completely away from what was going on at Rockfield. I think my job was really kinda trying to keep them believing in it and getting on with it and writing and playing rather than worrying about everything else that was maybe going on around them."

Which is precisely why a genius producer like Abbiss is so much in demand. The turmoil surrounding the inception of Kasabian's second album could have led to them imploding, but when it came down to it, the fundamental work ethic and sense of invention remained intact.

"I've seen the way Serge writes," continues Abbiss, "and it can be anything from he'll just sit with an acoustic guitar [and] pretty much form a song in a traditional way and then think about how he wants it to sound, or it might come out of a jam or it might come out of a two bar arpeggiated synth line that they just love the feel of and love the groove of and there'll be that and a drum beat ... there's lots of little ideas floating around the whole time.

We went in with an idea for about a dozen, and of them I'd say half were really well formed and we did what we needed to do [there] really, really quickly. It was like a massive relief for everybody, the band especially, and we literally went in and in the space of just [about] two weeks maybe, we'd finished six songs, and everyone was just really excited."

The relief to be working creatively as an unit together again was palpable. The pace slowed a little afterwards, but because the group had the residential studio booked for a good two months, they were able to build into the sessions some thinking time to work on the material.

"We'd try and do some work on this tune, and if it wasn't ready, me and Barn would just go back to London," continues the producer. "They'd carry on, on their own, for a couple of days without having the feeling that I was knocking on the door every hours going 'How's it going then?' So I used to make myself scarce! You know, they're grown-ups so if I said to them, 'Okay, well, I'll come back in three days' time, and just have a look at those couple of tunes and see what you've come up with,' so if they didn't want to work for a day, they didn't have to. It wasn't like teachers there going, 'Why haven't you done your homework?!' and it ended up being very productive actually. Because they wouldn't always do exactly what we'd talked about doing, 'cause they're creative people, so I'd come back and there'd be some amazing new tune that they'd done and they were really buzzing about, and that's fine with me! I don't care what they do as long as it's good."

It's also a hell of a lot of fun, and Kasabian were never averse to a bit of that. "It's pretty much two months of getting pissed and having a laugh with your mates and making music, really," says Barny. "Cause it's residential, you kind of settle in and everyone's there all the time and it was a real blast. Just good fun and how a record should be. We tended to not do too much during the day, and start work before dinner, have a break for dinner, have a couple of beers and see what happened. There was never really any agenda for work, which is really how it should be. Sort of, 'Let's have a crack at this, let's have a bash at this, let's try this,' sort of thing … it was just a lot of good fun.

I think all of Kasabian are big enough characters with all of us together not to need anything [in terms of entertainment, pool tables etc]. There weren't any PlayStations and stuff. Serge had a little studio in his bedroom we'd set up, so while we were down in the studio doing bits 'n' bobs, he could go up into his studio to work on things – so we had two studios running together. It was mainly evenings and night-times that all the stuff got done … somehow. It's not much fun waking up at 10am and going, 'Okay, do something brilliant!' You're just not in the mood, and that's the brilliant thing about being in a residential, you can just do it when you feel like, blast through stuff and get it done very quickly. And a lot of stuff was done very, very quickly, although there's a lot of hanging around not doing much. But when we did start working, we could easily [do] a track a night.

'The Doberman' was done in one evening. Most of the actual live band sort of tracks were pretty much done in an evening. It's just the way they play, the way they sound together. Ian's a fantastic drummer, one of the best that you can imagine. And for this album, because he's so solid, it just made the live recording an easier thing to do, because you've got someone just holding everything down. There were only a third of the tracks [finished], a lot of the others started with Serge with his stuff then we'd layer stuff on them and build them up in layers, and a few were just pretty much live takes."

The album was coming together brilliantly well, and it even had a title, which was inevitably thought up by the sharp-witted Tom Meighan, whose propensity for the odd but inspired, off the planet phraseology had not gone unnoticed. He'd already described his group's rise in terms of all sorts of weird and wonderful things including the Masters Of The Universe cartoon series in more than one interview and, according to Nick Raymonde, his knack for the epigram is one of the hugely endearing intelligence traits he and Kasabian possess.

"Tom is one of the funniest people I've ever met," beams Raymonde, "because he says things that are *totally* out of the context of human reality. They're comic book/Conan/Wagner-esque, almost, really dramatic ideas that he'll just come up with – in a word. He had these big words when he'd be describing something … and Serge would visibly recoil from the fact that Tom had managed to encapsulate in two syllables what he had spent four days in constructing the musical proposition of! Tom *got* what it was that they were making; he's not just the singer, [because] somehow [he's] able to sum up in one word what they are trying to do. And that is very powerful. Very interesting chap, Tom, because he could have been frightening. Wagner, in a sense, can be quite frightening if you're not ready for it. He'll go … perfect example … 'It's so *Empire*.'"[66]

So … Empire.

So.

Empire.

The sessions were cracking on at a great pace, and with most of the basic backing done it was time to look at additional musicians to bolster matters. The first track on the album is the Karloff/Pizzorno-penned title track, 'Empire', and its glammy/disco stomp features the vocal talents of Lithuanian vocalist Joana Glaza of the very excellent band, Joana And The Wolf. She happened to have been recording with Jim Abbiss on her own band's material, and the producer brought Kasabian down to one of her gigs at London's Water Rats venue.

"The funny thing is," Glaza explains for this book, "I'm so bad about remembering names that when I was introduced to them I was completely unaware who these guys were! I just thought, 'Uh, they must be some known band,' because everyone was whispering their name. And after the gig, my manager told me that Sergio really liked the gig and had called me a female Iggy Pop. I thought, 'Ah, cool, this guy really has some imagination because he is not comparing me to P.J. Harvey or Kate Bush, just like anyone else would.'

Then I was asked to sing on their song. Everything was organized through our management so I had no idea what sort of thing they wanted: did they want me to sing backing vocals or duet? I had no bloody idea. I only remember I was saying to my manager that I don't want to, or rather cannot, sing someone else's songs, if for example they'll tell me to, 'sing this or that', I'm only good doing my own stuff and so on. Now I realize how crazy and stubborn I must have sounded. And so one late evening after we had a meeting with Jim Abbiss to discuss our future recording of [Joana And The Wolf's] 'Purple Nights', Jim asked me if I want to give it a go with the Kasabian song that very evening, since our meeting was happening just in the next door pub to Olympic studios. It was almost midnight. I had a horrible cough but my senses whispered to me, 'Go ahead girl, you can trust this man, it's gonna be a beautiful adventure.' And so it was."

Jim Abbiss remembers the reference material the band were thinking of when they asked Glaza to add her input to the process. "We just had this idea of 'The Great Gig In The Sky' by Pink Floyd for her vocal, but that's a much more soulful vocal than what we ended up with, not that Joana doesn't sing with soul, but it's the kind of thing that was in our minds. It just soared off and went into madness, and she was good at that, although it doesn't sound anything like the Floyd tune!" As it turned out, Glaza told Jim and

Serge (who was also at the session), that she didn't want to hear any reference material, and preferred in fact to just let herself go with what was in her mind, with a little medicinal whisky added to take care of her cough, of course [67].

Her experience offers an insight into the value of a producer who can mesh into the creative process so easily, to allow things to happen almost organically – which is, of course, exactly the approach that made *Kasabian* turn out how it did.

"I found a wonderful harmony while working with Jim," smiles the Lithuanian lass. "Total freedom and direction all in one. He totally trusted me and let me go the way I felt was right. It's like I'm having a certain vision and he let me follow it. And when for some reasons I would lose my own path towards that vision, he would quickly notice that and direct me back on my way. He also made me feel very confident, so I could open up and be in my own world while singing. There was only Jim and Sergio there. Sergio was amazing. It was like meeting completely a different person. At the gig he was, you know, a cool guy, while in the studio he was transformed. He looked relaxed, inspired and curious, like a wizard in his own magic laboratory. They played me the song 'Empire', and it sounded more like a finished version. It was only then I heard it for the first time. There was this gap of forty seconds where they said they wanted me to improvise on.

I explained that I'm always good at spontaneous things, and since I really liked the song I got some ideas instantly and I didn't want to lose them or confuse myself with some other ideas on the top. I must say Jim Abbiss was amazing. He absolutely supported me, though probably someone else would think, 'What the fuck?' Sergio was supportive too, he was open-minded and it seemed he would let me try anything. Anything! Man, when you have so much freedom, certainly you are bound to create something very special. And so I took my little recorder and ran to the other room to record my initial ideas, being scared as hell that I might forget them. Then I came back and Jim suggested me recording it properly. They set the mic for me in the little room with the window to the main room, where Sergio and Jim were. And so I started my witch-like hysterical howls. Jim was there recording take after take. Each take was different. At least I tried to make them different! Later, Jim chose the best ones and layered them. At certain points, Jim said something like, 'How do you do that, can we see how do you make that sound?' And so he and Sergio squatted down to that little window and they looked for a while how I sung. And I will always remember it as the best compliment. It made me feel very special then. You know, me singing and them watching with faces full of amazement." As anyone who's ever seen Joana And The Wolf play live will testify, Ms Glaza is a very special talent indeed.

The album also features guest musicians on the track, 'Me Plus One', destined later to become a single. They are Algerian string players that Abbiss and pals had sourced in Paris. "When Serge came down, immediately before the album, two or three weeks before we started," Abbiss explains, "he came down to meet me in a little studio in west London, just to go through the demos, to talk about what we should do with them, so I had more of an idea of what we were going to do and stuff. He played me certain tunes and one of them was 'Empire', and one was 'Little White Rabbit', which became 'Me Plus One'. He didn't really know how to describe it, but he envisaged a string sound that wasn't a lush string sound, he wanted it sort of folky, gypsy, sort of Indian-sounding, potentially. I'd worked on some stuff with Björk many years ago and we'd used Indian string players, and so I went down this route of trying to find that, and it started to get very complicated!

I've done hundreds of ordinary string sessions and they can be great, but they can also be quite predictable and quite sweet sounding and that's the last thing we wanted, so we got on the Eurostar and went to Paris, and met up with these Algerians. It was just ludicrous really, but it was kinda fun, nobody spoke English, and I can speak about twenty words of French, none of which involve the word 'violin', but we managed to get through it by singing to each other, and laughing. We got the stuff done, and it was one of the funniest couple of days I've spent in a studio, and I think it sounds awesome, because especially on 'Me Plus One', it's not what you'd expect at the end of this summery folk tune, you don't expect these kinda gypsy strings to come in."[68]

Building in moments to allow inspiration to flow is important, says the producer. "I've heard this argument from some other producers, who say that they know exactly what they want when they go in the studio, and they come out with it, and I wish I was that good. It's never exactly what I think when I go in the studio because I don't understand how you can completely know what it's going to be. I think it's about going in with an idea of *sort of* where you're going. Obviously you know what you like and what you don't like, because I suppose more of it's about your own taste than anything else, the job of making records, and then it's about how you react to it not taking the path that's exactly what you thought it might. If it's nothing like what you said [it was going to be initially, then] if someone does something creative that [you didn't plan, then you should] embrace it."

Proof of this creative flexibility is the brace of tracks that end the album, the plaintive, Beatles-inspired and uplifting 'British Legion', which is all about making it through dark times, and the equally-atmospheric album closer, 'The Doberman'. That latter track has a lovely aspect to it that firmly places the influence back in the farm's nights spent watching Sergio Leone's Spaghetti Westerns, including a wonderful trumpet solo that is at once atmospheric and skilful.

"That track was sounding fantastic," enthuses Abbiss. "I had gastric flu and was a day late coming back after a break and they'd laid down the backing track of that with Barny really late the night before. They'd basically had this tune knocking around that they weren't sure what to do with, Serge kept changing ideas on it, and they just did a live take of it. I came back in the morning, and I was just blown away by this backing track, and I was like, 'That's amazing, let's not change that, that's really, really brilliant.' We did some overdubs, it became more and more 'Spaghetti Western sounding' at the end; we just were sitting around one night talking about what to do at the end of the tune, because it was already sounding pretty epic. I can't remember who said, 'Let's just get some Ennio Morricone trumpet on the end' but I had some videos of all the spaghetti western stuff and we watched *A Fistful Of Dollars* or *For A Few Dollars More*, one of them, and there was this amazing bit of trumpet in there. The band were like, 'That has got to be the end of this tune!' so we got some musicians down and one of them was a trumpet player. I made him a cup of tea and he said, 'What am I doing?' and I sat him down with the film and said, 'Just listen to this, something like this.' He just went, 'Oh yeah, okay, great,' came down to the studio, and in one take played what [is on the final track]. We all just looked at each other like, 'That's worked out a bit too well!' Because we were expecting two hours of saying, 'No, no not quite mate, just a bit more like…' and he literally played it in one take and it was amazing, a 'wow' moment."

It remains so.

They'd cracked it: setting up the atmosphere to allow the ideas to flow was the goal, and they had certainly succeeded. The new record,

Empire proved to be an album that had strong nods towards the electronica that underpinned swathes of *Kasabian*, but with a more – shudder – *mature* and traditional, disciplined songwriting approach. As second albums go, rarely has there been one that has been beset with potentially band-threatening trouble at its inception, and rarely has there been one that has answered every question that was asked of it so firmly and confidently.

CHAPTER EIGHTEEN

World Cup Year

Aside from album sessions, 2006 brought with it a whole slew of publicity, including a rather odd announcement in May that Serge was to hook up with Armani as their new 'face', with that fashion label even providing the group with clothes to wear. The band also played in the Celebrity World Cup Soccer Six event during that month, representing Italia, of course, beating Justin Hawkins-led England side in the final of Sky TV's tournament (having beaten the likes of the *Hollyoaks* cast on their triumphant march to success). Tom had time to wind up a few people in print, too, telling *NME* later that the *Hollyoaks* lot were "arrogant little pricks."[69]

Aside from the disastrous World Cup campaign for England, Kasabian also lost out on a Brit award once more, this time being pipped in the 'British Rock Band' category by Leeds' Kaiser Chiefs, who were named after a South African football team featuring the legendary Doctor Khumalo. For Kasabian's part, they'd recorded a version of David Bowie's classic track, 'Heroes', which was used throughout the tournament as part of ITV's coverage of the unfolding competition. Ian Matthews, perhaps in homage to Rooney's pre-World Cup injury, had damaged himself playing squash, and as a result had to play the bass drum with his left rather than right foot on the recording, which was still more or less done in one day.

"There might be a lot of Bowie fans that might not be too happy with what we did," Matthews mused, "but we had to keep it upbeat because it was for the ITV football – for people scoring goals and fans going wild, getting behind their country and everything. We did an upbeat version which is only like twenty seconds. It was fun. David Bowie gave his thumbs up [too], which was even better."[70]

The early part of the year had been spent in the studio, which obviously meant that the band was itching to get out there and play again. And that meant bringing in a guitarist to at least cover the holes that the absent Karloff would usually have filled with his unique, Flying V-taught, whizzbang six-string madness. This time, however, there was a more or less ready-made replacement, and someone who not only understood what the music was about, but a character who had shared the touring madness with Kasabian the previous year as part of the band, Mad Action. His name was Jay Mehler.

"He's amazing," enthuses Ryan Bernstein, bandmate of Mehler in Mad Action and subsequently the offshoot group Ty Cobb. "A great human being in every sense. He's my best friend. Paul [Cobb, the other member of Ty Cobb] and I, he's our third guy. He couldn't be a closer friend to me. A great friend. I sound like a Hallmark card! But he's by far the funniest human being I've ever met, he keeps everyone smiling, you know what I mean? Above all of that, he's as talented as they come as a musician. They spent a lot of time with Jay on tour with us, that's how they met him and he's just a great guy. They probably had that moment where they were like, 'Wow, we need a guitar player' and they thought of Jay and they asked him. It's pretty simple. I'm sure they probably had other people in mind but he's an amazing musician and they love the guy so it kinda made sense for them to ask him." So they did and, as they knew would happen, he fitted in very well into the live set.

And so it was that Kasabian hit the summer festivals with a renewed sense of destiny within their hearts. They were getting excited, as the public was, about the new material, too. "When the first single comes out," Serge said, "people are going to be asking, 'What the fuck are these lads on?' It's all about the tunes. It's just a classic record and that's the exciting thing. That's exactly why I wanted to be in a band."[71]

Though Glastonbury was taking a year off in 2006, the boys were firmly in gigging mode, so it was soon to become obvious that there had been a line-up change. The official press release about Karloff's departure came after much online speculation on July 17. "Lead guitarist/keyboard player Chris Karloff and Kasabian have parted company," it read. "Karloff and the band experienced certain creative and artistic differences during the writing and recording of their second album. These irreconcilable and diverging approaches resulted in the band asking Karloff to leave the group. Karloff will pursue a musical career elsewhere."[72]

Indeed he would, and people who have heard Chris Pratt's newer material rate it as being on a par with the aesthetic of *Kasabian*, with a distinct electronic bent but also featuring mighty guitar lines and melodic elements. "Chris' solo stuff is a lot more like the old stuff," explains Neil Ridley. "Quite riff-based but with quite an electronica edge to it. He's still as focussed as he ever was. His plan was to try and put a few bits and pieces together; he had some demos that I heard a while ago that sounded pretty exciting. You get the feeling that he'll land back on his feet again at some point. Chris was doing some stuff with one of the guys from Death In Vegas (the one based in New York) and the singer from The Shining, which was the band of Duncan Baxter, ex-bassist of The Verve." It surely won't be too long before he re-emerges, and when he does he can count on some support from his old compardres.

"He's clever and he's good enough to do anything he wants," concluded Tom in an *NME* interview. "He knows I've got his back and I'll be there when he wants to do something else in music."[73]

One of the last tracks Karloff co-wrote with Kasabian was the first, long-awaited single to come from the new album. *NME* magazine immediately made it 'Single of the Week', as it shot straight into the charts at Number 9. Its video was again directed by the talented Wiz, and continued on the military theme, this time casting the band as the Eleventh Hussars Regiment made infamous for the Charge Of The Light Brigade. Again, it deals with the lot of the ordinary soldier fighting in a war not necessarily of his own making, and is as atmospheric and epic as the track itself. It is a massive statement of intent from the band, and if anyone still had doubts about the band's fizz and fire, they were assuaged indeed by the single. The video debuted exclusively on Channel 4 on July 24.

"We believed in [Wiz] and his perspective," Serge told *Chart Attack*, "and kind of trusted him with all that. The actual video making process was really fun, what with the costumes and all the sets. We're supposed to be these soldiers in a bunker, meant to be there for ages, we're stuck. And out comes this little lad with a message from the general, but he doesn't get there, does he? And that's the last straw, so we decide, 'Fuck this!' and we start marching away. And then we get blown to shit, don't we? And Tom still keeps on marching!"[74]

Two days later, the group headed into the studio with Zane Lowe for his Radio One show, performing a full set for broadcast.[75] The pace, as ever, was relentless, with August 3 seeing a 'secret' gig in London recorded exclusively for play on MTV, and then a couple of gigs that would bring notoriety even to the outspoken Kasabian. Having snagged support slots previously with inspirations The Who – a band that are often credited by members of Kasabian as being one of the first groups to integrate keyboards and synths into rock 'n' roll – the Leicester lads were to hook up with none other than the Rolling Stones, supporting the wizened rockers at gigs in Zurich and Nice on August 5 and 8 respectively[76]. Make no mistake, the Stones are a massive deal, and their career over forty-plus[77] years of music spans nearly all the influences that Kasabian share. The tour was to promote the new Stones LP, *A Bigger Bang*, which was by no means named after the sound that Keith Richards made when he hit the ground after falling out of a palm tree in Fiji earlier that year. Hilariously, Tom Meighan, in an interview on Channel 4, inadvisedly let rip about the ticket prices of the gigs, and his outburst has become one of the legendary moments in rock interview history, even by his own excellent standards.

"It's quite incredible," he said. "We're fucking supporting them! So if we get kicked off the stage we've got to buy a ticket, which is about 200 quid. It's probably Americans who are running it, not Jagger. And Richards isn't going to know what's fucking going on, is he?"[78] After being politely informed that, as the support band, Kasabian would have to do nothing of the sort, an official statement was swiftly made, saying that the band were, "incredibly honoured and excited to be supporting the Stones on some of their European dates – it's like a dream come true for all of us." No harm done, and a funny story to tell the grandkids at least. Tom was later to proclaim the experience as "fucking magic."

"Yeah, it's very virtual," he told talented interviewer Lauren Tones of Gigwise.com, inventing another rather excellent adjective. "It's not real really, it's just strange. When Mick Jagger came up to us and gave us a hug, yeah, it's wonderful … amazing … and the fucking shows are unbelievable. It's massive! A proper fairground stage, mate!"

Kasabian's August was as busy as ever, with appearances at Ibiza Rocks in Bar M on that magical island followed by Edinburgh, Brixton and Dublin. The Ibiza appearance was heavily supported by Noel Gallagher as a concept. "He said it's the final piece of the pyramid for us," commented Serge. "It'll be a case of lock all the doors when we get to the Manumission villa! We're not staying at Noel's [Ibiza villa]. Everyone's maddest friends are coming out so it could get messy, and we wouldn't want to do that to the man."[79]

The band once again made a mark with their performance of 'Club Foot' being aired on *The David Letterman Show* on August 19, the same night that the group were wowing Chelmsford audiences at the V Festival. The album was about to be released, and early reviews were already coming in, *NME* magazine rating it 9/10 and drooling that, "Through sheer, bloody-minded belief, weapons-grade stamina and a big, big imagination, Kasabian have willed themselves into brilliance."[80] In celebration, Serge promptly got himself on the Sky TV show, *Soccer AM*, and reminded everyone of his previous career plan by scoring an absolutely brilliant volley. Seriously, go find the clip online and be astonished ...

Rolling Stone magazine were a little more sniffy about the record, calling it "artless pastiche" and "miles worse than their shallow but tasty first [album]." Which was rather churlish of them, but it didn't stop *Empire* rise inexorably to the top of the UK charts on its release. The band were also becoming tired of the constant references to Madchester and baggy, which were continuing to come even given the glam rock tendencies of *Empire*.

"This record is just more live-er (sic)," mused Meighan. "There's more of a heartbeat to this record than the first one, you know, the first one was more choppy and really aggressive and really hazy and really kind of pot smoking kind of scene, you know? This was like, you can tell we've been on the road for a bit and the songs are more constructed. What I reckon it was, people put us in there with The Stone Roses ... but now we're turning into a Led Zeppelin-like rock and roll band. We've never been a part of a baggy scene or anything."

"It's just shit journalism though, mate. If anyone's read the right reviews in *Uncut*, or fucking *Q* or *NME* or whatever ... they'll know it's just shit journalism, I hate it. It's shit. They are shit; they are shit at what they do. We're not fucking Happy Mondays! We're not fucking keyboard music; it's got nothing to fucking do with it. You know, Shaun Ryder ... all they did was fucking do dance beats, man. We're more than that, give us credit, for fuck's sake. You know, I love the Mondays. But come on, the fucking Stone Roses only had one fucking album you know ... I'm not dissing it, the Manchester scene is amazing and I love it and I love all them bands but we've never been anything to do with them. None of them. Like 'The Doberman' and songs like fucking 'Seek & Destroy' and 'British

Legion', I don't get it; you know, it's weird. Look at our single, 'Empire'. We're possibly the only band apart from Radiohead that changes tempo with a new single we've put out and no band dares do it, you know. We're like a futuristic Led Zeppelin, man, with strings on, electronic on it ... it's lazy, man, it's fucking rubbish."

Empire is also extremely significant for its artwork. It features merely the title of the record and the name of the band, and not a masked man in sight. This is, and was, a deliberate ploy to distance themselves from the connotations that their previous artwork had brought, and in any case 'Stealth' was hardly a word with which a million-selling act could describe themselves.

"The artwork on the first record is about gang mentality," explained Tom. "It's based on us coming to town, being in the city and the initial thing of us growing up together as a union, that was the first record on the sleeve. This one we had to change, I couldn't stand that military stuff; we just seen a pack of cards and it looked cool."

Ian Matthews elaborated on the point. "We went through a few ideas and some were quite hideous. It was just like, 'Yeah, there's another album with a man on the front, Oh God, yeah, same again,' you know what I mean?" It is this constant urge to explore different aesthetics that is at the heart of much of what the band does, and which will serve them well as they continue building the Kasabian empire far and wide.

September was no less eventful, with their return to Leicester recorded once more by old mates XFM, before a performance at NME.com's tenth birthday party, at which they were joined by Noel Gallagher for 'The Doberman' and 'Club Foot' at London's Koko on September 12. Gallagher subsequently proclaimed the band as on a par with The Prodigy and Primal Scream, and also communicated his pleasure at catching up with the Kasabian boys, after the extremely hectic schedules of both bands had meant they'd not seen much of each other of late. September 19 was the release date for DJ Shadow's new album, *The Outsider*, which was all the more ironically named from a Kasabian point of view, as it featured both Serge and Karloff on the track, 'The Tiger'.

There was also the small matter of recording a brand new video, for the forthcoming single, the hugely catchy, big-balled, glam rock stomper, 'Shoot The Runner'. The directors this time around were Parisian duo Alex & Martin, who had won a Grammy award in 2005 with their video for U2's 'Vertigo'.

"I think, for me, they are very creative," explained Martin Fougerol for this book. "And they are creative even with their image. They take care of their image, they like the image and the band is very interested about their image and the contact [we had with each other] was very cool. That's why we were very free to do it [in terms of being given a free hand] until the end. For me, the track is an amazing track and you know when you trust the band and the band trusts you something good happens. It was a very good experience and it's always a very good experience to work in that way."

Fougerol was very pleased when the duo were asked to work on the video, which was designed as a performance clip – uniquely, being the first time that Kasabian had actually committed to a straight performance. The rushes would then be taken and treated in post-production, psychedelic colours overlaid in a technique known as Rotoscoping, to produce a decidedly 1960s feel to matters.

"It's like *Yellow Submarine*, something like that," continues the video director. "Even the outfits, we were inspired because the singer has the kind of jacket like John Lennon in *Yellow Submarine*. They just did a rock performance, we shot with two cameras in HD, and we made a special outfit for the band to separate the colours. So the band was very ridiculous during the shoot because the outfits were very flashy like *Sesame Street*, just to separate the colour for the post-production. Even for the face, you know, we did a ridiculous and very ugly make-up job, the moustache, the beard and the eyes. Just to do a simple key in post after that. During the shooting, we had a lot of fun with the band, it was very amazing to shoot it. There was two parts of the shoots. First we shot the performance then afterwards we made a hundred bowls of paint and threw the bowl on the band. In real life." So the explosions you see behind the band are of real bowls of paint, rather than extras added in afterwards.

"At the beginning, we were a little bit afraid because we did some tests, we were a little bit afraid to throw too many bowls on the band – we didn't want to hurt the band. I remember it was a nightmare because they were obliged, for safety, to have big glasses on their eyes like a painter. Protective glasses, and we were obliged to erase the glass, and blah blah blah. Too much work! You can feel with certain shots in the video, like when the singer shoots his gun, with his hand, you get another shot when he has the bullets in the back. We edited like that but it was very, very exhausting to do it 'cause we threw some big bowls of paint, and it's a little bit weird for a band to do that. Quite violent, you know, and some guys in my team had so much pleasure in throwing the paint! I remember the singer was, 'Hey, Hey, Heyyy!!' and my guys were Bom! Bom! Bom! Bom! Bom!" Lots of fun; the video went down exceptionally well and was soon all over MTV, *Q*, *Kerrang!* Hits and The Box in the UK.

Back to America, then, and a secret MySpace fans-only show in Providence was followed up by a performance of 'Empire' (the single), again on *David Letterman*. With the eyes of the world firmly back on Kasabian's music and visual aspect, it was something of an inevitability that there would be a press interview that was both provocative and, in its own way, playful. By now people had come to expect Kasabian's confidence in themselves to occasionally manifest itself as broadsides across the bow of 'lesser' bands, and they didn't disappoint this time either as Meighan railed against an entire musical style, that of emo. Anyway, he begun by saying that contrary to the received wisdom that the genre was bringing teenagers together, it was a negative force as it just engendered a negative attitude that led to one hell of a lot of teenage whinging.

"It may upset people," he told *MTV*, "but emo is dead in my eyes. Fuck emo. Just enjoy the world," he continued. "Teenagers are better than that, man. I want to tell them to be positive about life. You've been brought up well by your parents, so don't sit around in your bedroom cutting your wrists. Grow up."[81]

In the same interview, the singer also looked forward to the imminent American return, saying that the band had unfinished business to take care of in the States, where they were still something of a cult band rather than the huge force for musical good that they planned to be one day. And, indeed, they were doing everything in their power to make it happen, including a photoshoot with Mick Rock for *Playboy* magazine. Thankfully everyone kept their clothes on as it was for a forthcoming issue of the magazine concentrating on new, hip, and sexy talent.

With the band on tour once more, they would have been cheered by the announcement that *Empire* had been nominated in the 'Best Album' category of the 2006 Q Awards, and the video for the title single flagged up in the 'Best Video' section, which would be voted for by viewers of the channel. On Kasabian's return to the UK, however, they would have been equally pissed off when they found out at the ceremony on October 30 that the 'Best Video' went to The Killers, and Sheffield tykes the Arctic Monkeys ran away with the award for 'Best Album', having had their own phenomenal rise during 2006 to celebrate. Still, Oasis were named as 'Best Act In The World Today', so the beers were flowing freely even if a major award continued to elude the Blaby boys.

There had been an astonishing performance on October 28, 2006, when The BBC Electric Proms featured Kasabian performing reworkings of their tracks alongside the BBC Concert Orchestra.[82] The Electric Proms version of this age-old festival took place at the Roundhouse and other Camden venues, and was dedicated to creating new musical moments. In Kasabian's case, it was a triumph: their set also saw none other than Zak Starkey, son of Ringo and sometime drummer of both The Who and Oasis, climb behind the kit for three songs. It was, to say the least, Empire.

"Kasabian's mission to make each gig a celebration saw another conquest here at the Roundhouse this evening," gushed the BBC site. "They more than pulled off their ambition to perform with a full concert orchestra and turned the venue into one huge party. By the time the band close with an epic version of 'L.S.F.', it's hard to know who's loving it more – the crowd or the band. 'It's been fucking monumental!' declares lead singer Tom Meighan as the band have a group hug and depart. The entire crowd continue to sing the final track's chorus as they pile out of the building and into the Camden night."[83] As audiences had been doing since the very first Kasabian tours, in all fairness: it's just that the profile had got bigger.

A week later, November 2, the band played alongside Noel Gallagher at a drugs benefit event entitled, 'For Pity's Sake, Focus' which raises money for Focus 12, a charity that deals with drug addiction in all its forms. Noel played a full set, as did comedian Russell Brand, whilst Tom and Serge ran through acoustic versions of various Kasabian tracks.

November brought little respite from the schedules either, with the band first fitting in a three-song set for Richard Bacon's XFM show on November 3, then an acoustic session and oodles of banter for Jonathan Ross on BBC Radio Two, before heading to France briefly for a live appearance on Canal Plus on November 7, and finally in this whirlwind of session activity, an always-enjoyable meet up in Radio One's 'Live Lounge' with Jo Whiley the following day. There was even time for a couple of days on the video shoot (more of which later) and to enjoy their appearance on *Jools Holland* and *Top Of The Pops 2* on November 10 and 11 respectively,[84] before the band hopped back on a plane to America to complete that leg of the tour. Exhausting, yes, but ultimately worthwhile. Somewhere amidst the absolute maelstrom of activity, 'Shoot The Runner' was released, hitting Number 14 in the singles charts. The DVD video, in common with the video for 'Empire', reached Number 1 in the DVD video charts. Another strong performance to keep things ticking along nicely whilst the year began to draw to its close, bolstered even more by a semi-official white label mix of 'Me Plus One' that was ripping up the dancefloors in the clubs once more.

It had been put together with his usual aplomb by Jacques Du Cont of Les Rhythms Digitales, hugely famous for their 1999 album, *Darkdancer*. Less well-known in some circles was the fact that the talented Jacques himself was born Stuart Price, the electronic funkster notably donning several different nomes des plumes for his various projects.

Kasabian might not have won many awards during the year as a band, but Sergio Pizzorno was soon to change that as he was named in *NME's* completely arbitrary annual 'Cool List'. Serge came in at number 21, a rather unimpressive statistic.[85] It is, really, only a bit of fun, and an excuse for that magazine to trot out old facts, bits of gossip and stories about the people concerned, as well as remind everybody that these are groups who might be worth listening to. The Kasabian website, in its marvellously sardonic way, commented thus.

"This makes him 'one' cooler than Eugene Hutz (Gogol Bordello), but not quite as debonair as Jamie Frost from The Automatic. He also neatly dissects the White Stripes; less suave than Jack, but more urbane than Meg. Well done to him though. Apparently he gets a sew-on badge which he's going to attach to his P.E. kit next to the 25m swimming award."[86]

There was just time to slot in a ten-date UK tour before Christmas (sadly the gig in Sheffield on December 22 had to be cancelled after Serge developed a viral infection), and as had become customary, it was a triumphant celebration of a year. This was reiterated on December 27, when *MTV* dedicated a whole night to the band, who, let's not forget, had barely released their debut album some eighteen months previously. The sun had well and truly risen over the empire.

CHAPTER 19

A One-Way Ticket From Here To Eternity, And Back

2007 began with Kasabian revisiting the land of the rising sun, with another series of gigs in Japan, a country that had always been enthusiastically behind everything the band had done. Here, the status of Kasabian is truly that of superstars, with their press conferences almost as well-attended as the gigs themselves. The band loved it there, Ian Matthews offering that, "Japan is completely mind-blowing and the Japanese are completely mind-blowing people."[87] Cosmic.

"They are *so* famous among people loving UK rock music," says Japanese fan Yuri Yamafuji. "But many Japanese people know only the name or don't know totally them – most of their fans have all their albums and some fans also buy their singles. *Kasabian* was ranked 17th in the general ranking, and 5th in the overseas ranking. *Empire* was ranked 8th in the general ranking, and ranked 3rd in the overseas ranking. I think most of Japanese love going to their gigs."

Immediately after that leg of the tour, Kasabian jetted off to Australia and New Zealand, the first time the band had ever played Down Under, thus meeting a new set of fervent fans. The Aussies in particular were ready for the band's streetwise vibe and earthy, approachable blokey-ness, having grown up, amongst others, on a steady diet of all things AC/DC. And, of course, it being summer over there, it was also a chance for the band to get out of the rain and wind awhile too.

Mark Vidler was also up to his old tricks, with a couple of brand new mash-ups of the band in his locker. "I'd done a couple of ones that aren't official," he says. "'Bus Stop Runner' which was pure homage to The Sweet and Slade, I mean, it was … so sublime. That's why I put them with The Hollies, I thought that'd be interesting 'cause I'd always liked that particular song, and with them being a more Northern band and that, it all sort of tied in. I had a lot of fun with that, it was cheeky. I then did 'Breaking My Bloody Process' which was Kasabian, My Bloody Valentine and The Music thing afterwards … That was good as well, quite a few people picked up on it, a few DJs said, 'Yeah, I dropped this at the weekend and it got the indie kids going', which is good. I don't know if the band got to hear the other two, probably, you know they're all quite closely-knit so I'm sure they would have heard it but they certainly didn't write me any nasty letters!"

The *Playboy* link-up continued with the news that the group would be designing some T-Shirts for the magazine's fashion label, along with Flaming Lips.[88] Other acts contributing designs to the 'Rock The Rabbit' range included Metric, The Thievery Corporation, Stellastarr★ and Soulwax. The original T-shirt designs would later be auctioned off for the music-affiliated AIDS charity, Lifebeat.

The Aussie and New Zealand gigs were part of 'The Big Day Out', a rolling rock festival somewhat akin to Lollapolooza, and Kasabian, despite being on the second stage and often playing mid-afternoon, were on top form. "On the Green Stage, Kasabian were making their Perth debut," wrote one reviewer, "and the UK band certainly proved their worth. Opening with current single, 'Shoot the Runner', the band alternated between songs from UK number one album *Empire* and their 2004 self-titled debut ('Reason Is Treason', 'Sun/Rise/Light/Flies', 'Processed Beats'). They saved the best for last though, as they invited Jet singer Nic Cester on stage to help out with backing vocals on 'L.S.F.' at the end of their set."[89] Which, of course, the crowd went home singing …

"A mid-afternoon highlight," wrote *Central Station*, "was UK-band Kasabian (playing on the Green Stage) who fused rock and electronica in a fresh and funky way. With a very English 'pop-rock-meets-house' sound and a lead singer who swaggered much like Liam Gallagher, the band really impressed. The music was new to most but memorable!"[90]

Back home, it was time to release the new single, 'Me Plus One'. Different formats variously offering the addition of a cover of Jefferson Airplane's 'Somebody To Love' from another Radio One 'Live Lounge' session, a Jacques Le Cont remix of the title track, and a dip into the recent archives too, for a track from way back in the Jacknife Lee session days. "It was 'Simple Plan,'" recalls Lee. "This became 'Caught In Her Mind' and was one of the ones we put strings on."

'Me Plus One' also featured an outstanding piece of visual art that is, in many ways, one of the most enlightening videos about the ethos of the band and what had happened to them over the last two years. It was again directed by Scott Lyon, who'd kicked off the visual aspect with his work for the band's 'Reason Is Treason', the pseudo-political, mysterious, revolutionary collage that had such an impact in the early days.

"It was funny meeting up with them again," beams Lyon. "Compared to meeting them in the pub when nobody had heard of them on the first single, [then] when I met them again they were a big band. It was good to do another video with them, definitely.

I had a few conversations with Serge about it, and it started off with an initial thing from Serge that he wanted quite an element of black magic and voodoo which had come from a Rolling Stones aftershow he'd been to. He said it was this fucking crazy party; all decked out in a kind of black magic way with real snakes, really dark and kind of opulent, lots of velvet curtains and marble pillars. As you probably can imagine, it was rather debauched with loads of beautiful women there, and rock stars, and he was saying, 'There's a bit of black magic in there, particularly with the orchestration in the track.' You can hear that, where the track goes a bit psychedelic, a bit almost Ravi Shankar-mystical. There's that kind of air about it. And when he said that I said, 'Yeah, I can see what you mean, I can see how that kind of fits with the track.' But then I didn't want it to turn into a Guns N' Roses video, that was my worry. I said to him, 'I understand what you mean, candles and curtains and stuff, but I don't wanna be 'November Rain',' and it was thinking of a way of introducing it."

So the pair cooked up a narrative where the video begins, in black and white, in a post-gig dressing room. The band is exhausted after playing, but buzzing with adrenaline. The viewer sees that the backstage area is dull in comparison to what they have just been through, as the band doodle with guitars and look at the floor.

Suddenly, however, things change: the black and white internalised near-claustrophobia explodes into an ethereal room full of naked, dancing girls who initially appear in the shape of the famous Dali Skull.

157

"You know, if you're going down a kind of voodoo route, you've gotta watch it," continues Lyon. "A lot of videos go down that route and it doesn't really work. So I started to think, 'It needs to be approached in a slightly more conceptual way and it can be a little bit more artistic how the performance happens, where the people are, and what we were going to do with the girls, and forming them into the Dali skull shape and having them moving about, and stuff.' And just creating something that is a purely visual thing, the mood of it fitting with the music and integrating in some performance, not performance with instruments 'cause that wouldn't have worked, them performing with naked girls wouldn't have worked. It would have worked for them! We were just trying to create something that had the right [vibe] for the track and create something that was visually quite interesting.

To add to the mystical feel of matters, the video was shot in an old Masonic Hall that had been previously bricked up for a century and subsequently rediscovered by accident. On such discoveries are truly memorable creative ideas borne.[91]

'Me Plus One' reached Number 9 in the UK charts, a more than decent start to a year that promised much, not least when the *NME* award nominations came around again on January 30. This time around, Kasabian were up for four gongs: 'Best British Band', 'Best Live Band', 'Best Album' and 'Best Video' (for the single, 'Empire'). As had become more or less par for the course, the band's main rivals were the likes of Muse, The Killers, My Chemical Romance and Arctic Monkeys.

The Sheffield lads were favourites of Kasabian and Tom Meighan would regularly big them up in the press. "I remember talking to mates about them before they were signed," he told *Starpulse*, "and now look at them. That guy's a poet and I'm a proper fan of everything they're about. It's fucking amazing for British music, what those lads have done."[92] Which was rather nice, because My Chemical Romance had got rather shorter shrift from the frontman in more than one interview, the Kasabian ethos being diametrically opposed to emo bands, who, in Kasabian-land at least, portrayed a self-indulgent misery that echoed somewhat the whingey ethos of a certain section of grunge fans who'd missed the point entirely several years previously.

"It's like ventriloquists' music," said Meighan. "It's weird and dark. They don't have anything positive to say. The only good news is that it won't last. These clowns won't be around for much longer. Their make-up will flake off and the scene will die out. And it can't happen soon enough."[93] Needless to say, My Chemical Romance themselves responded by thanking Kasabian for the compliment. Which showed a fair sense of humour, at least. Perhaps their widely-lauded album, *The Black Parade*, selling near-ten million copies helped them stomach the criticism.

February saw a rash of live appearances across Europe, the band keeping the profile up despite missing out yet again on a Brit Award (Arctic Monkeys won the 'Best British Group' gong for which Kasabian had been nominated, which was becoming rather a familiar tale). But something rather excellent was just about to happen, not least the lads storming open the *NME* Shockwaves Awards ceremony with a two song-set of 'Empire' and 'Stuntman', but later in the night, for the first time ever, being brought back onstage with Noel Gallagher. And it wasn't to play alongside him, either. The band had *actually* won an award for a change, for 'Best Live Band'.[94]

"This is the first award we've ever won," yelled a jubilant Tom. "So about fucking time!" He went on to offer his thanks, and in his usual direct and eminently quotable way, he'd hit the nail on the head. The band deserved recognition for their three years of hard work and knocking down walls on their quest to attain widespread success in music, and this was a long-overdue gesture of acknowledgement.

March 29, 2007 was the date of another unique performance, with Kasabian part of the week-long shindig that comprised a set of concerts in aid of the Teenage Cancer Trust. Noel Gallagher, Scouse legends Shack and hotly-tipped act The View started it off on at the Royal Albert Hall, Shack and The Coral supporting Noel the next night, with Wednesday being a comedy gig with Noel Fielding and Russell Brand. Kasabian's gig on the Thursday, alongside The Bees and The Lea Shores, was a highlight of the week which also featured Kaiser Chiefs, Gruff Rhys and The Cribs on the Friday night before the whole kaboodle was brought to a magnificent end by The Electric City, Vincent Vincent And The Villains and headliners The Who. As fundraisers go, you couldn't wish for a more perfect blend of the contemporary and classic rock acts, and the week of gigs showed the masses of talent that the UK could boast. Kasabian ended with 'L.S.F.'

After the footy season finished, the festivals beckoned once more, including an appearance at the Green Energy Festival at Dublin Castle (the actual castle in Dublin, not the tiny venue in London) on May 5, whilst Serge was pondering new musical avenues constantly.

Though *Empire* was still in the middle of its shelf life, being a prolific chap he was constantly working on new material, as well as thinking a little more laterally about artists with whom he'd like to hook up.

"If I could write for any artist," he said, "it would be Alicia Keys. "I think she could be the next Aretha Franklin but unfortunately she's just stuck with gold chains around her neck."[95] The group were on superb form, hitting the stage at the Radio One Big Weekend in Preston on May 19 to delirious mid-afternoon response, dedicating songs to The Twang and recent tourmates The Fratellis. May and June saw the boys travel the length and breadth of Europe, enjoying festival hospitality everywhere from Spain to Romania, two great adventures that book-ended their return to the place which, perhaps more than any other, had launched their career into overdrive back in 2004.

Glastonbury.

And this time they would be on at approximately 9.15pm as main support to Arctic Monkeys on the famous Pyramid Stage, on Friday 22 June. The cycle was almost complete; in three short years they'd jumped from being cool-underground group whose rising status put them on as very first act, opening the festival, to performing whilst the sun went down over what Meighan would probably call the by-now *extremely* monged revellers. And, of course, they let nobody down.

"From the first note of 'Shoot The Runner'," wrote *The Guardian*, "through to the Hacienda-lite of 'Processed Beats', Kasabian are the consummate festival band, providing enthusiastically encouraging singalongs and frequent bouts of furious flag-waving."[96] And though the reviewer sounded a note of caution, feeling that the band's propensity for elongating the grooves at times in the songs was worryingly proggy, the overwhelming vibe was a positive one. The band themselves weren't able to hang around with their headlining mates the Arctic Monkeys, however, because they were booked on a flight to a Romanian festival imminently after their performance.[97] Tom did find time to encourage people to do what people do at festivals, however, exhorting the crowd at "the best festival in the world" to, "do as many drugs as you like, find the nearest puddle and swim in it."[98] The only downside to beset the group at Glastonbury was when Noel Gallagher had to pull out of a planned surprise spot onstage with the band in favour of prior studio commitments with Oasis that were unable to be rescheduled.

The next huge gig, festivals aside, was an appearance at Live Earth on July 7, 2007 (07.07.07, numerologists), a monumental statement of unity by musicians, fans and those concerned with the future of the planet that brought together some two billion people via satellite link-ups and live concerts, to raise awareness of the growing climate crisis worldwide. Twenty four hours of music across seven continents would serve to show the massive support for actual action to be taken to begin to respect the planet more, from the individual, personal small lifestyle changes such as not leaving electronic devices on standby right up to the presidents, prime ministers and politicians charged by the people with the responsibility to represent them. A media event, of a sort, but one with which nobody could seriously disagree. And anyway, apart from anything else it meant that the lads got to play at Wembley Stadium, albeit not entirely in the way that they'd envisaged as youngsters kicking a ball around the Blaby streets all those years ago.

"Kasabian," wrote Kitty Empire of *The Observer*, "provided the day's first blast of grubby, insolent rock 'n' roll. Their command of that precious rock resource – energy – was impressive, as 'L.S.F.' rumbled along seditiously. If having drums like little earthquakes counts, they are an environmental force to be reckoned with." [99]

The band's gig at Somerset House in London on July 13 was no less impressive, reviewers enjoying the day out in the sun as much as the magic and the music on offer. The band, who hit the stage around an hour late due to numerous unavoidable technical factors, were introduced by one of their celebrity fans, the actor Danny Dyer. [100] *The Independent* reviewed the concert and, despite expressing some misgivings about the lads' "opaque" lyrics and a set that had remained relatively static for a year or so, could not help but admit that this was a band who you couldn't ignore. "I'd seen Kasabian on other occasions and been underwhelmed," they said, "but tonight's gig was something else entirely: the aural equivalent of five men storming the Bastille." [101] Which you could say is quite an opaque way to talk about a musical concert, but there you have it.

The band was now calling a few shots, and gleefully took an opportunity to settle a few journalist scores in typical style. "Tom and Serge were together at [a festival] when they came into do interviews," laughs Eddy Temple-Morris. "It was one of those junket tents, you know, like a press tent. And they're always heaving with journalists, websites, TV, radio and that. There was this sort of murmur, 'Kasabian are coming, Kasabian are coming in,' and the whole place was packed and they come in with their arms around each other and it was like, bluebottles to a turd.

Everybody crowds around them and thrusts microphones in their face and I was just hanging back, not wanting to get in the way. And they stopped and they sort of waved all the microphones away. And then Serge looks at me and goes, 'Motherfucker!' and Tom goes 'LEGEND!' and they stop everybody and go, 'Listen all you cunts, you listen to whatever that guy over there says,' pointing at me, 'because he was there for us right at the beginning and all you cunts weren't, so we're going to talk to him and then maybe we might talk to you if we're in a good mood about it, if we're feeling all right. And whatever he says, you fucking listen to him.' It was just so sweet." The good will out, sir.

Excitingly, the band sloped off to the beautiful Ibiza for the now-annual *Ibiza Rocks* festival, which brought indie and rock revellers over to the notorious party island for a series of concerts in venues usually more suited to lost souls, such as the gargantuan Manumission nightclub in the tourist-hellish surroundings of San Antonio. The boys had blown the roof off Bar M there the previous year, and were in their element again at the same venue on July 16 and 17, kicking back during the hazy day and kicking up a storm overnight, with old sparring partner Zane Lowe broadcasting his radio show from the venue.

The summer was notable for some new releases, first up being the *Saturday Sessions* CD, a collection of tracks from Dermot O'Leary's show on which Kasabian ran through the aforementioned 'Pictures Of Matchstick Men', the Quo track that not only had more than three chords but also featured rather a psychedelic edge to it. The group's July 31 appearance at the iTunes festival with Dead 60s was also recorded and subsequently made available as a downloadable release. Tom found time also to lend some backing vocals to fellow Leicestershire musician, Jersey Budd, the highly-rated songwriter who was recording his new single.

"Tom's a legend," Budd enthuses. "He came down, we were round at Serge's house the week before having a bit of a drink and [at] about two in the morning [I asked Tom], 'Do you fancy coming down and doing some backing vocals?' and he couldn't wait to do it. He jumped at the chance, really. Bless him, he came down, didn't ask for no money, just beers and fags, and he just did it straight on. Genius, really.

I had a melody in my mind and I [showed him it]," continues Budd, who in a previous guise had been in a band with Tom's elder brother, John.[(102)] "He said, 'Yeah alright' and he sang his melody and there was no comparison really, know what I mean, he's like a whirlwind, he comes right up and it was two hundred miles an hour, he were gone within forty five minutes! That was it. Coming in, doing it and off he goes to do something else. When someone comes in from the outside … I've listened to it over and over again and he comes in from the outside, fresh ideas and – bang! – away you go."

Excitingly, there soon came the news that there would be a brand new Kasabian single/E.P. in the offing. It was the first new material from the band in a long while, and it was also completely self-contained in terms of the writing and recording process.

"This was done in my house in a little room downstairs," explained Serge. "Just in front of a computer, I produced it all myself. Because we're just doing all these festivals we thought, 'Why don't we just put one out and crack on?'" He went on to explain how he was in a very verdant period as far as songwriting was concerned, which was good news to the ears of fans who were beginning to wonder exactly when some brand new songs would appear. It duly appeared on the radio and as a download, although to date the planned CD release has not happened. But it grabbed the attention of more than a few magazines, and the reviews were very promising indeed.

"They've gone mod!" enthused Q. "The lead track from this month's brand new EP mixes the spirit of early Kinks with the flash of Austin Powers. Luckily they won't need to change their wardrobe."[(103)]

As usual, the singer was great value for money, telling XFM Manchester that the EP was just a limited edition for the fans, to show everyone that the group were always on the move and not just sitting on their arses playing PlayStation and watching *Happy Days*. "It's a vital track and a vital time for music, and I think we've done a great job of it," Meighan noted, before claiming that the band were working on tracks for a brand new album, and that it was, "shaping up like a bowl of jelly, and it sounds like an owl at night time."[(104)] On the evidence of 'Fast Fuse' at least, it sounded like neither of those things: the classic rock elements even more in evidence on a track that was as live-sounding as the band had sounded in some time. There was also a very inventive appearance on Mark Ronson's album, *Version*, which took contemporary tracks and re-interpreted them in a different style. Alongside the likes of Lily Allen, who sang a version of the Kaiser Chiefs' 'Oh My God', and Amy Winehouse performing The Zutons' 'Valerie', Tom and Serge guested on a

163

lounge jazz reworking of their own 'L.S.F. (Lost Souls Forever)' to great effect. The concept could have been rather clichéd, but because it was delivered with a mixture of respect and mischief, it was actually one of the best releases of 2007.

There was great news once more in September, with a nomination from Q *Magazine* as 'Best Live Band' (in the event, Muse won it), as well as Tom Meighan splashing the cash a little bit, as he purchased the original bicycle which was used in the film, *E. T. The Extra Terrestrial.* The singer was subsequently spotted by several people flying through the night skies in silhouette against a lover's moon, with a strange bundle of wrapped-up goodness in the front basket. Maybe.

As the new football season kicked off in earnest, it also came to light that Norwich City F.C. would be running out to 'Club Foot', which is quite apt really when you think about it. Modelling came back onto the radar once more, this time with Tom being named as a face of Gio-Goi, modelling alongside both Liam Gallagher and Welsh actor Rhys Ifans, who got his cock out in *Twin Town,* but kept it inside the classy clobber this time.[(105)]

Kasabian found time to lend their weight to the growing campaign round the re-release of the Sex Pistols' classic, 'God Save The Queen' during October, which was to come out to coincide with the punk legends' tour to celebrate the thirtieth anniversary of *Never Mind The Bollocks.* "I'm going to be buying a few copies," said Serge. "I think it's a great idea to try to get it back to Number 1."[(106)] He also noted that the group were still inspirational to many people and that the band often listened to the Pistols in their dressing room before gigs. Kasabian also threw their support behind an auction of sixty-two signed Gibson guitars, with the proceeds of the subsequent auction to be shared between Nordoff-Robbins Music Therapy, The Prince's Trust and the Teenage Cancer Trust.

There was more recording news in November, with Serge alluding to sessions taking place in his new studio, a converted shoe factory, towards the end of 2007. It's a good set-up, with oodles of equipment both new and vintage, and because it has a great live room, it is a facility that allows the band to record live drums and instruments to a high standard. As 2007 drew to a close, Kasabian would spend more and more time there, laying down ideas and refining demos to a stage where they could bring in the production team once more and begin the sonic jigsaw process toward their new album in 2008. Tom kept himself busy when he had time off, first finding himself in an impromptu pub singalong on Boxing Day, 2007, duetting with Tara Simms on a rendition of 'Hey Jude' at her gig in the Black Horse, Leicester. The frontman also spent the best part, reportedly, of eight grand on life-size replicas of *Star Wars* characters C-3PO and R2-D2 to keep him company when he was at home; fantastically, he also gave an interview where he offered up the fact that he was going to call his first-born offspring 'Apollo Creed', which is quite brilliant, especially if it turns out to be a girl.

There was time only to fit in a raucous Hogmanay appearance in Edinburgh, the band seeing in the New Year in some style with a great set during which Noel Gallagher appeared, as if by magic, for three tracks. The set ended with an expensive, and exceptional, fireworks display, capping a year of total triumph.

As they have proved time and again, Kasabian are a band whose whole career is testament to the power of being creative, the power of dreams, of pulling each other through the hard times and the good alike, but more than that, having a damned good time doing it. Long may it continue to be so.

CHAPTER TWENTY

A New Hope

"The very odd thing about music is … it's very peculiar … when you are seventeen-years-old, you can go out to the local recreation ground on a Sunday morning and play football for the local team. And you can enjoy yourself and have a great time, without thinking, 'I'm better than David Fucking Beckham. I should be playing for Real Madrid.' You go out there and play, and you just enjoy yourself, you know you're not very good but you're alright. The converse of that is that you cannot go and play on a stage in a pub aged seventeen and enjoy yourself unless you think, 'I'm better than fucking Kasabian, I should be on Top Of The Pops.' And so there's millions of kids out there who think they're wonderful, when in fact they're not. I mean, it's a very rare gift, being one of those great groups. So it certainly empowers the same kids who give out demos, and do this and do that. Every town in Britain has a thousand bands. And nine hundred and ninety-five of them are shite; four of them are okay, and one of them will go on to change the world. And that doesn't change."

The late Sir Anthony H. Wilson, November 2006.

The impact that Kasabian have had on music is undeniable. Born to a backdrop of boredom, they injected the vibes back into rock, making it acceptable once more to go to gigs for the sheer *fun* of it. To get mashed up and dance with your mates. They'd lost members along the way, for sure, but one thing the band are is resilient, and also brave: to follow the hugely successful eponymous debut with *Empire* was a move that few expected them to make, and even fewer might have advised. As it stands, however, their self-belief has more than borne itself out.

As is the nature of music, everyone speculates about what the future might hold for a band whose career has been built on a mixture of true creative inspiration and a hugely impressive work ethic. "I don't think they're the kind of band," observes engineer Simon Barnicott, "where you really worry about what you have to do next. It'll just naturally just be something good, I don't ever think that's really a consideration."

Indeed it is not. Eddy Temple-Morris, the DJ who did so much to help the lads out in the early days, fighting their corner to get airplay, sees the future as rosy, and that is, he says, because of their musical background. "There's an obvious parallel which is Primal Scream," he says. "Primal Scream constantly reinvent themselves and that's what I see Kasabian doing. And that's why I see them as having longevity. Serge is a brilliant songwriter, Tom is a brilliant frontman and they are a sort of Glimmer twins in the old sense of the word. They're the Jagger and Richards, but back when they were good, when they were making really cool psychedelic records. They'll always have that fanbase and, because they'll keep reinventing themselves, they'll always pick up new fans with each album so they'll be a constant turnaround that'll keep things fresh."

James Barton is someone who knows a thing or two about both dance music and rock. As the founder of the super-club Cream, his group is now promoter of the UK's premier dance festival, Creamfields, as well as several other festivals including Liverpool Music Week. He sees Kasabian's career as being based on the strong fanbase that allows the band to constantly pursue different musical ideals. "Radiohead might be a good example of an artist that's got an amazing fanbase, that will sell thousands and thousands of tickets without breaking a sweat and will sell millions and millions of albums but don't have the big singles and the big commercial crossover record. And maybe that's what's in Kasabian's head, they don't want to be number 1 on *Top of the Pops*, they want to sit in the Top 3 in the album charts for two years; I think that's what their direction is. And again, like Radiohead, they've got an amazing live following. I think that Kasabian has got a bigger fanbase than what people are really aware of and I think that they've actually got a slightly bigger fanbase for when they play live than when they buy records. Because I think when they play live, they're just fucking great whoever you are and whatever you like, they will not fail to get you jumping up and down if you're in a venue watching them."

Producer Jim Abbiss makes the point that one thing about the music that Sergio Pizzorno produces is its blurred boundaries, and he comes back to name-check Sergio Leone's Spaghetti Westerns as an example.

"Even though it's called *The Good, The Bad And The Ugly*, it's never clear cut [which is which]," he muses. "What I like about both the characters and the music is that no one's actually all one thing and I think there's a kind of mystery to each character, there's never a conventional hero and again, that's something in his music: there's always a slightly unusual twist, it's never just straight ahead.

There are so many bands that are one thing, and you can define them in a neat three or four word soundbite – their first album, their songs will all be very similar, and you can pinpoint their influences. I don't think you can say that with Kasabian, they're kinda the antithesis of that. I think all their albums will be a massive mixture of things that turn them on at the time and they're into a lot of different sorts of music and that's what their next records will be like, [ever] more disparate, and more bonkers and more epic than the last one."

Kim Dawson, whose 'Playlist' column in the national newspaper the *Daily Star* is a very influential place for bands to be seen, thinks that it is the dynamic between Tom and Serge that makes Kasabian work so well. "Unlike most bands where the frontman does the writing, it's an interesting dynamic which appears, to those on the outside, to work. You can't take your eyes off Tom at a gig. He radiates effervescent rock characteristics. He's like a preacher and the fans are his disciples. He says, 'C'mon' and, 'God bless' about a hundred times during each show and it never becomes annoying, only part of his schoolboy charm. [But] Kasabian is Serge's band for sure. He clearly harbours a desire for the spotlight himself but [I think] vocally he's not as strong as Tom. That didn't stop them releasing 'Me Plus One' as a single with Serge on lead. I'm partial to 'Test Transmission', another Serge lead." To each their own, of course.

"It's gonna go stratospheric," declares Pete Oag of Little Ze. "I could always tell at the time, it was pretty obvious. I've met Noel Gallagher quite a few times and Oasis credit Kasabian for getting them to raise their game. Cause after they played with them in Benicassim two or three years ago, Oasis went on just after them and Noel couldn't believe how much they needed to raise their game. Just 'cause of what they're doing. I imagine they'll do Knebworth in two or three years, they'll just keep getting better and better I think. And they have got the tunes, they just sound absolutely massive … it's madness, absolute madness, taking that dance rock thing to another level. It's very uplifting; that's what their massive appeal is as well, it's feelgood music. As well as being pop, it's also cool and it's feelgood music as well. It's got everything."

Neil Ridley thinks the band have it in them to move into more proggy territory, and sees them as yet to write the album that will become known as their classic record. "I think that the band are capable of writing a modern day *Dark Side Of The Moon*, given a bit more time to experiment with things. As bands go they're the sort of band that, in terms of what they've done live, it's phenomenal. From a band that started out from humble roots but with aspirations of greatness, for them to be doing Alexandra Palace, inevitably they're going to be doing bigger and better shows but it's where they want to take it now. Inevitably you're going to make comparisons with the likes of Pink Floyd or any of these early pioneers of the scene and it takes a long time for it to be crystallised into one moment of greatness. I think that across the records that they've delivered now, you can hear moments of where this could go and it's a really exciting time for them I think. It could be a *Dark Side Of The Moon* Part II, but a little less long and inward facing."

"Obviously," offers Ryan Glover, "it's how much Tom wants to start getting involved with songwriting, but if Serge keeps having the inspiration that he has and keeps on producing the diversity of the tracks, I don't see why they can't continue to produce more great albums. Obviously the first album was new at the time, it was all slightly different. There was this raucous energy and the big attitude that they've got with the songs and onstage, but obviously there was also that modern touch to it, with the non-manmade sounds and stuff, the mellotron and all the samples they used whereas the second album was more of a band. It's hard to tell, if you're a diplomat, there's two ends of the scale. But from someone who's obviously been there on the first album and someone who's obviously witnessed their rise, so to speak, and as a musician, I probably would see it carrying on. Simple as that."

As for Nick Raymonde, a man who was highly influential in the signing to BMG in the first place, looking back at the success the band have had, he sees it as being a time that was more or less star-crossed. "I think it honestly was a magical combination of things that all happened, not by chance but where you thought something might work, and it did. Which doesn't often happen. A lot of serendipity; the simple thing of going, 'You need somewhere to rehearse' and finding not a pigsty – but a farm. It's like, you gave someone a little hint of an idea and they went off and turned it into a planet. That's what I think they've been extremely good at, and the other thing about them was that they were massively open to suggestions.

They wanted to be huge. But it wasn't even 'We want to be' – it was 'We're going to be', without being arrogant. Which is a very hard thing to do. You have to be the right person to get away with it. If I said it, you'd be, 'Uh, yeah, that's very interesting, Nick'. But there are certain artists that can go, 'What I'm doing is going to be huge. It will be huge.' And they convince you from a perspective of divorcing their self away from their ego. Maybe it's a part of their ego that drives the artist in them and maybe those who are very enlightened can divorce their self from their ego. Someone like David Bowie is a great example. He had that ability, where every time you read an interview with him or saw him interviewed, he seemed incredibly humble and intelligent and talked about his music like it was almost someone else doing it. And I think that Kasabian have that quality, and I think that's real superstar quality – when you hear somebody talking about themselves like it's a different person.

The people like Kasabian, it's not like they're 'driven', I wouldn't even call them 'ambitious' – [some] say they have a naivete but I don't think it's naivete, it's a hugely optimistic view that what they're doing is *really great*, that *they fucking love it. So why wouldn't you?* It's a sort of football analogy to me. It's like, Chelsea are brilliant, why wouldn't you support them?[107] Of course they're gonna win this game. Then when they lose, that fan may well be in tears – not because he's sad that they lost, but because he's devastated that he could have been wrong. But that's what they're like, they're into football, they go to the game believing they're gonna win. It's not bravado. And I think a lot of successful groups or artists are like that. And if they fail, it's absolutely devastating for them – for about a second. And then they do it again, and they keep on doing it even when everyone's saying, 'Stop!' But there's more to come and it's clear to me that Serge will still be making music in fifteen, twenty years time."

Shine On, you crazy diamonds … the story is just beginning …

Footnotes And All That

1 See end-note 2 in *Bruce Dickinson: Flashing Metal With Iron Maiden And Flying Solo, Shooman. J (Independent Music Press, 2007 ISBN: 0-9552822-4-1)*

2 Radio Nottingham interview, June 2004 as archived at
http://www.bbc.co.uk/nottingham/music/2004/06/kasabian_interview.shtml and accessed
October 2007

3 http://beehive.thisisleicestershire.co.uk/default.asp?
WCI=SiteHome&ID=8354&PageID=67432 retrieved November 2007

4 http://www.isnakebite.com/interviews/kasabian.html retrieved November 2007

5 Ibid.

6 Ibid.

7 For the uninitiated, the Flying V is a guitar so-called because of its distinctive shape (like a
sideways letter V). It's played mostly by metal guitarists, whose penchant for subtlety is hardly a
strong point. You're more likely to see Corey Beaulieu of Trivium shreddin' out a solo on one
of these Gibson-built babies, and for the young Pratt to play one in his Oasis/Stereophonics
inspired early bands was something of an incongruity. However, never look a gift horse in the
mouth; its design lends itself to guitar histrionics and it is therefore not a bad beast to learn
your chops on.

8 In homage to horror film actor Boris Karloff, whose real name was William Henry Pratt.

9 He elaborates: "There was another band called Perfume who got limited chart success but
kind of faded away, a band called Shwmf, with no vowels, and they were very good but they
split up as well. There was a band called The Haze, sort of Fun Lovin' Criminals stuff, and a
band called Monkey Egg too. Those bands were the most popular in Leicester at the time."

10 *Rip And Burn Magazine* interview, March 2005

11 *Big Issue* interview, January 29, 2007

12 At the beginning of this track, Tom mutters something. Scott Gilbert: "I was talking to the
headphones, 'Are you ready, Tom?' and he said, 'Alright mate, yeah.' That track's really
Stereophonics, you can really hear the progression on them."

13 Scott Gilbert, again: "I remember taking the piss out of Chris and saying, 'It's Stereophonics!'

14 The practice of grabbing studio downtime to record, or in this case, to mix, young bands'
initial efforts means very cheap studio time when anybody sensible is probably in the pub, or
at home wrapping up their presents. Iron Maiden famously recorded their legendary
Soundhouse Tapes on New Year's Eve 1978, for example.

15 www.aekituesday.com/2005/02/22/band-we-like-kasabian-interview/ - retrieved October
2007

16 Scott Gilbert will bear witness to the number of hopefuls who have not progressed to make
a career.

17 Ben Kealy proved impossible to track down for this book despite all best efforts.

18 *Rip And Burn Magazine* interview, March 2005

19 Ben Cole remembers: "Tom came over," laughs the journalist. "I don't know why but he
came over to tell me how shit the band that they were supporting were, so the pair of us
went up and gave them some grief. Basically they were like a Cast covers band, they were
from Liverpool and it showed. At the time I was a crappy lazy journalist and if I didn't like
something I'd just slag it off. I think Tom and the band quite liked that, it was all part of the
egging-on."

20 They are, nobody should ever take drugs, ever, ever. They are very bad and naughty and no creative art has ever been ever influenced by the concept of altered states. And Samuel Taylor Coleridge, Wordsworth, Shakespeare, Rimbaud, Dylan Thomas and their ilk were all gainfully employed as accountants. And so were The Beatles. Don't do it. Just say no.

21 Do not under any circumstances go and buy ten more copies of this book, immediately.

22 As a name, it's up there with Slartibartfast isn't it?

23 And this would be a rather spurious footnote, which it is.

24 *Rip And Burn Magazine* interview, March 2005

25 http://www.pollstar.com/news/viewhotstar.pl?Artist=KASABI Interview, July 2005 and retrieved December 2007

26 Nick Raymonde: "It was just an outbuilding, I don't even think there was a toilet in there."

27 This is not a negative comment but rather refers to the spaces in the arrangement that, by design and by chance, allow for a little injection of energy from a particular instrument, sound or player. In this case, Mitch refers to drumfills and rhythmic figures that he was able to introduce to enhance the vibe of the piece of music.

28 Now only semi-ironically renamed 'Paradise Studios'.

29 "I was travelling down from Portsmouth to Leicester," expands Mitch Glover. "Darting in and out of the country with my main band Kosheen, going out and coming back with them then going out and coming back with [Kasabian] so it was all a bit back and forth. I did some sketches at the farm, where they were based, then we did the sessions with Jacknife Lee, and some more at Metropolis in North London, but that was without Jacknife and just with the in-house guys and the band, basically ...
The guys were in and out [of the studio] quite a bit so I was just getting down there when I could.
I did more gigging with them than anything; the recordings were in really short blasts, the band were working quite quickly so I was getting a lot of stuff done quite quickly. I spent a fair bit of time in the studio but it was more in rehearsals and gigs where I spent most of my time."

30 http://www.isnakebite.com/interviews/kasabian/kasabian3.html retrieved November 2007

31 Jacknife Lee's production on that third Snow Patrol LP, *Final Straw* helped gain the band and himself huge and widespread acclaim, the record peaking at Number Three in the official UK Charts, winning Ivor Novello Awards and selling two million copies to date. Garret subsequently won two Grammy Awards for his production work on the U2 album, *How To Dismantle An Atomic Bomb*.

32 http://www.excellentonline.com/article.php3?story_id=1313 interview, February 2005 and retrieved November 2007

33 Men? What have men got to do with it?

34 http://www.eyeballkid.com/xfm_remix_night_live_review.htm retrieved November 2007

35 As quoted on Kasabian's press release for the 'Club Foot' single, April 2004

36 Dan Stubbs interview, 2004

37 *Clash Magazine* Interview, February 2004.

38 I wonder if that works for authors too? Hmm. The evidence so far would suggest otherwise.

39 He says "technically his home town" because, as he told me, "I'm a Portsmouth boy but where I lived had a Southampton postcode, if you come out of my room you have a signpost and you've got left – Portsmouth and right – Southampton. So where I lived was actually smack bang on the borderline. Only a mile and a half up the road but you change to a PO postcode but everyone said I was from Pompey, it's where I was born and bred and I always say Pompey, I prefer Pompey than Southampton. I'm a Pompey supporter." A very, very important distinction, albeit one that Harry Redknapp has a little trouble with on occasion.

40 http://www.excellentonline.com/article.php3?story_id=1313 retrieved November 2007

41 www.dirtyzine.co.uk/content/view/29/2 retrieved November 2007

42 www.nme.com/news/kasabian/17211, 16 June 2004, retrieved November 2007

43 Widely reported in March 2005 including: http://festivalwise.com/news.asp?id=5603 retrieved November 2007

44 www.virtualfestivals.com/latest/interviews/1153 Interview, June 2004 and retrieved November 2007

45 With thanks to Matt Cartmell.

46 www.festivalwise.com/news.asp?id=5603 retrieved October 2007

47 *Bullit* Magazine Interview, June 2004

48 With thanks to Matt Cartmell

49 With thanks to Hannah Hamilton

50 With thanks to Hannah Hamilton

51 Hoare expands: "In Bristol there's basically two drummers in my opinion that are just *killing* and that's Ian Matthews and Clive Deamer (who plays with Portishead and Robert Plant and others). Ian would look up to him. They're both capable of doing all the styles, and fusing them at once as well, which nowadays is exactly what you need to do, because basically music's like that now. It's a fusion of all styles, everything's going in there and that's why I think he's so relevant now as a drummer."

52 John Hoare: "We started in the school jazz band and did various jazz gigs over the years, we played with Jamie Cullum which was a one-off that Ian did. I used to play with Jamie regularly but Ian did a one-off gig in Bristol with him, that was fun!" Ian Matthews' first forays into serious bands, however, were the equally technically taxing but polar opposite: he cut his teeth playing in various heavy metal groups whilst in school.

53 Vidler feels it worked because it was so coherent, and rather than people picking up on it being merely a blend of two dynamic, driving, tuneful tracks, it was effectively a new song. "The best ones work on that third level, you know the meeting of the two individual tracks and becoming new, and in this case I think it worked so well. I must admit, I did laugh when the two blended together, the first time I heard it I thought, 'Oh, this could be special!' It's funny, I was going to do the B-Side and I was just going to do it backwards like the Stone Roses used to do, I thought, 'I'll just record the whole thing backwards' but it didn't make it to the pressing plant in time so it was just a one sided white label! It was the case that I just sort of reversed the whole track and called it 'Processed Waterfall' – spelt backwards – just as a little homage to what the Roses used to do [most famously on 'Don't Stop', which is 'Waterfall' played backwards with new vocals and overdubs added to create a new song.] I don't think it was ever officially released. It came out on vinyl and went through so many pressings on half inch records, initially pressed up a thousand but I think they ended up pressing about five or six thousand, it did actually chart, in the dance charts it was in the Top Ten or something in the second week of release. I was just seeing it everywhere, in everybody's favourite list of this, that and the other. It was quite hot at the time, it got me a bit of extra work on top of that so it was quite nice!"

54 http://www.freewilliamsburg.com/archives/2005/01/kasabian_interv.html retrieved October 2007

55 www.aekituesday.com/interviews/kasabian/ January 2005 interview, retrieved October 2007

56 Ibid.

57 http://www.freewilliamsburg.com/archives/2005/01/kasabian_interv.html retrieved October 2007

58 The setlist for the tour: I.D. / Cutt Off / Reason Is Treason / Processed Beats / 55 / The Nightworkers / L.S.F. (Lost Souls Forever) / Club Foot

59 Mad Action played several gigs alongside Kasabian during March 2004 in the UK.

60 www.timmcmahan.com/kasabian.htm retrieved November 2007

61 www.virtualfestivals.com/latest/interviews/1153 Interview, June 2004 and retrieved November 2007

62 Meighan also admitted to hiring an Obi-Wan outfit to wear around The Farm previously.

63 http://www.vh1.com/artists/news/1510328/20050926/kasabian.jhtml retrieved December 2007

64 www.rollingstone.com/artists/jet/articles/story/7683844/kasabian_swim_with_oasis retrieved November 2007

65 Widely reported at the time and now another legendary quote but sourced November 2007 from www.live4ever.us/2005_12_04_newsroomarchives

66 Tom Meighan told *MTV*: ""We called the record *Empire* [because] we've been using the word for many years now to describe things we think are great: a pair of shoes, a pair of boobs, a good CD – that *is* Empire"

67 Joana Glaza: "This whisky story seems to be a widespread legend already! Well it's true that on the way to the studio I asked Jim if we could buy some whisky. The thing is I was coughing. Did you ever try to sing while coughing? That's quite impossible. So I was worried if I get those coughing attacks while recording. It was too late for any pharmacy anyway. When I asked Jim to buy me Bells he was like, 'You're not gonna drink this horrible whisky, let me buy you a good, proper one.' But I was very insistent that that is the one I needed. Well, after recording, for a while my cough did come back me so I had to sip that magic Bells." Not exactly conventional, but you can hardly argue with the results – and Lithuanians are wonderful people.

68 Joana again: "Can you tell now which lines I sung while still sober and which after a little bit of whisky? I bet you can't. Cause you don't need to drink to feel drunk, those Moroccan (sic) strings they were using were more than enough to make your head spin around. And that is a great part about their music it takes you to the different level."

69 *NME* interview, July 8 2006

70 www.acedmagazine.com/kasabian_interview.htm retrieved October 2007

71 www.nme.com June 6, 2006, retrieved October 2007

72 www.kasabian.com July 17, 2006

73 *NME,* September 9, 2006

74 www.chartattack.com/damn/2006/12/2202.cfm retrieved November 2007

75 The setlist was: Empire / Reason Is Treason/ Sun/Rise/Light/Flies/ Shoot The Runner / Cutt Off / By My Side /Last Trip (In Flight) / Processed Beats / The Doberman / Club Foot / Stuntman / L.S.F. (Lost Souls Forever)

76 Kaiser Chiefs supported the Stones in Croatia, it was The Charlatans in London and Glasgow, and Guns N' Roses at Nuremburg and Leipzig.

77 Also the title of a very fine magazine, apparently.

78 http://stereogum.com/archives/kasabian-insults-apologizes-to-mick-and-keef_003062.html retrieved November 2007

79 http://www.contactmusic.com/news.nsf/article/gallagher%20convinced%20kasabian%20to%20rock%20ibiza_1004090 retrieved October 2007

80 *NME*, August 23, 2006

81 http://www.mtv.com/news/articles/1541950/20060928/kasabian.jhtml Sept 29, 2006 and retrieved November 2007

82 See footnote 16.

83 http://www.bbc.co.uk/electricproms/2006/kasabian/ retrieved November 2007

84 Kasabian were also on MTV and T4, whilst Soccer AM were using the band's cover of the Status Quo track 'Pictures Of Matchstalk Men' over their goals round-up segment that weekend. The band had initially recorded the track for a Dermot O'Leary session on Radio Two, and it appeared as one of the B-sides of 'Shoot The Runner'.

85 That's *The Moon Nightclub* in Milton Keynes, not the big thing in the sky made of cream cheese that was the inspiration for the popular 1969 smash hit TV movie, 'Moon Landings',

starring the likes of Neil Armstrong and 'Buzz' Aldrin, produced and directed by NASA and filmed in the Nevada desert.

86 http://www.kasabian.co.uk/news/331/-/36/ retrieved November 2007

87 www.acedmagazine.com/kasabian_interview.htm retrieved October 2007

88 We refer to the fine band fronted by Wayne Coyne.

89 www.fasterlouder.com.au/reviews/events/7765/ retrieved October 2007

90 www.centralstation.com.au/articles/shownews.asp retrieved October 2007

91 Scott Lyon: "There's a hotel next to Liverpool Street Station called Great Eastern. It got renovated about seven or eight years ago, and whilst they were doing that they knocked a wall down and found these big wooden doors that led into this Masonic temple. It's actually underneath the hotel. It was immaculate, it'd been walled up for 150 years and nobody knew about it, so they had to get in contact with the Masonic lodge about it. They said, 'You can't do anything to it – you can use it if you want to hire it out or something, but you can't change it , it has to remain like that.' It's quite an amazing room, I've always wanted to shoot something in there but I was waiting for the right thing to come along. And when this came along it was straight away my mind went, 'That's it, let's go, it's got to be shot in there.' It's a mad place. It's amazing, it's got this weird, weird room and as soon as you go in there you know funny stuff's happened in there! There's a lot of funny signs, and symbols, and old chairs and robes and that kind of thing."

92 www.starpulse.com/news/index.php/2006/02/13/kasabian_praises_arctic_monkeys retrieved October 2007

93 Widely reported, but sourced from http://www.nme.com/news/kasabian/24719 retrieved July 2007

94 'Best British Band' was won by Muse; 'Best Video' went to the Killers; 'Best Album' was scooped up by, oops, Arctic Monkeys.

95
http://www.contactmusic.com/news.nsf/article/kasabian%20dream%20of%20collaboration%20 with%20keys_1030581 retrieved December 2007

96 *The Guardian* live review, June 23 2007

97 The set: 'Shoot The Runner' / 'Reason Is Treason' / 'Cutt Off' / 'Me Plus One' / 'Empire' / 'I.D.' / 'Last Trip (In Flight)' / 'Processed Beats' / 'The Doberman' / 'Club Foot' / 'Stuntman' / 'L.S.F.'

98 I should write lyrics for Grange Hill anti-drugs songs, I'm wasted here. In every sense.

99 *The Observer*, July 8, 2007

100 Other rumoured celeb fans include Arnold Schwarzenegger, who apparently would work out to the first album, and William Shatner, who certainly did dance to them when they were on the same TV show. Both these people were contacted for quotes for this book, for a laugh. Neither replied.

101 http://arts.independent.co.uk/music/reviews/article2783529.ece July 19 2007 and retrieved November 2007

102 His group, Invagold, had supported Saracuse in the early days.

103 http://home.q4music.com/cgi-bin/q50/track.pl?id=168 retrieved November 2007

104 http://www.xfmmanchester.co.uk/article.asp?id=450644 retrieved December 2007

105 It might have been his brother's waggling about, I can't remember. I didn't really look too closely.

106 www.nme.com retrieved December 2007

107 Cause they're rubbish and nowhere near as good as Bangor City?

Discography

ALBUMS

Kasabian – Kasabian: *Club Foot / Processed Beats / Reason Is Treason /I.D. / Orange / L.S.F. (Lost Souls Forever) / Running Battle / Test Transmission / Pinch Roller / Cutt Off / Butcher Blues / Ovary Stripe / U Boat / Reason Is Treason (Jacknife Lee Mix)*
CD – Paradise 16 / Sony BMG 2004

Kasabian – Kasabian DVD+ Edition: *As above with the addition of: Reason Is Treason Video / Club Foot Video L.S.F (Lost Souls Forever) Video / Making Of Club Foot Video / Making Of L.S.F (Lost Souls Forever) Video Field Of Dreams (Shot At Farmstock Gig in May 2005)*
Dual Layer CD/DVD – Sony BMG 2005

Kasabian - Live From Brixton Academy: *I.D. / Cutt Off / Reason Is Treason / Running Battle / Processed Beats / 55 / Test Transmission / Butcher Blues / The Nightworkers / Pan Am Slit Scan / L.S.F. (Lost Souls Forever) / U Boat / Ovary Stripe / Club Foot*
Download only. Recorded on December 15, 2004 – Serge's 24th birthday, fact fans.

Kasabian – Empire: *Empire / Shoot The Runner / Last Trip (In Flight) / Me Plus One / Sun/Rise/Night/Flies / Apnoea / By My Side / Stuntman / Seek & Destroy / British Legion / The Doberman / Rick's Tune (Hidden Track)*
CD – Paradise 39 / Sony BMG 2006
10"Vinyl – Sony BMG 2006

Various editions have different bonus tracks, by country as follows:
US: Ketang / Heroes / Empire (Video)
Japan: Stuntman (Live)

UK: XFM Live Session: Shoot the Runner / Reason is Treason/ Empire / The Doberman / L.S.F

Kasabian – Empire CVD/DVD
As above with the addition of a DVD featuring: 'Empire' Video / Documentary / Making Of 'Empire' Video
CD/DVD – Sony BMG 2006

Kasabian – Empire (Instrumentals)
Promo CD of instrumental versions of the album. Ever wondered how MOTD etc manage to get such great loops? Here's part of yer answer…
CD Promo - Paradise Records / Sony BMG

SINGLES / EPS
(Official releases in various formats)

Club Foot: *Club Foot (Single Edit) / Club Foot (Jagz Kooner Vocal Mix) / Sand Clit / Trash Can / Club Foot (Paradise Mix)*
Club Foot (Reissue): *Club Foot / The Duke / Bang / Club Foot (Jimmy Douglass Remix) / 55 (Live From Brixton Academy)*
CD / 10" – Paradise Records / Sony BMG 2004 / 2005

L.S.F. (Lost Souls Forever): *L.S.F. (Lost Souls Forever) / Lab Twat / Doctor Zapp / L.S.F. (Jagz Kooner Mix – Radio Edit) / L.S.F. (Jagz Kooner Mix) / Club Foot (Live At The Cabinet War Rooms)*
CD / 10" – Paradise Records / Sony BMG 2004 / 2007

Processed Beats: *Processed Beats / The Nightworkers / L.S.F. (Live At The Cabinet War Rooms) / Processed Beats (Afrika Bambaataa Remix) / Ovary Stripe (Band Remix)*
CD / 10" – Paradise Records / Sony BMG 2003 / 2004

Cutt Off: *Cutt Off (Single Mix) / Processed Beats (Acoustic Live Lounge Session) / Out Of Space (Acoustic Live Lounge Session) / Beneficial Herbs (Demo) / Pan Am Slit Scam / Cutt Off (Mad Action Remix)*
CD / 10" – Paradise Records / Sony BMG 2005

Empire: *Empire (Single Edit) / Black Whistler / Ketang / Empire (Jagz Kooner Remix)*

CD / 10" – Paradise Records / Sony BMG
2006

Shoot The Runner: *Shoot The Runner
(Clean) / Shoot The Runner (Album Mix) /
Shoot The Runner (Shakes Remix) / Stay
Away From The Brown Acid (Part 1) / Shoot
The Runner (4 Music Presents)*
CD / 10" – Paradise Records / Sony BMG
2006

Me Plus One: *Me Plus One / Me Plus One
(Jacques Le Cont Mix) / Me Plus One (Jacques
Le Cont Dub) / Somebody To Love / Caught
In Her Mind (Paradise Remix)*
CD / 10" – Paradise Records / Sony BMG
2006

iTunes Festival EP: *Shoot The Runner /
Empire / Stuntman / The Doberman / Club
Foot / L.S.F. (Lost Souls Forever)*
ITunes Download Only recorded at July 31,
2006 gig at ICA, London.

iTunes XFM Empire EP: *Shoot The
Runner / Reason Is Treason / Empire / The
Doberman / L.S.F. (Lost Souls Forever)*
iTunes Download Only UK release

Fast Fuse: *Fast Fuse / Thick As Thieves*
10" Promo, Digital Download, CD Promo
(Japan) – Columbia 2007

SELECTED COMPUTER
GAME APPEARANCES

(Various console and computer formats)
*Ten years ago you wouldn't even have had a
section like this in the discography, you know.
And in ten years time it'll quite possibly be the
biggest bit. Even Sex Pistols re-record tracks for
this sort of thing these days, which is hilarious.*

FIFA Football 2004
(aka FIFA 2004, FIFA Soccer 2004)
*'L.S.F. (Lost Souls Forever)' features on the
soundtrack of the third greatest soccer game ever
made.*
Electronic Arts, 2003

Sony PSP Launch Disk
*W.I.Z.' video for 'Club Foot' features on this
free disk that shipped with initial copies of the
PlayStationPortable.*
Sony Computer Entertainment, 2004

Gran Turismo 4
*Racing game, featuring 'Reason Is Treason' in
the intro as well as on the in-game soundtrack.*
Sony Computer Entertainment, 2004

Pro Evolution Soccer 5
*'Club Foot' appears on this iteration of the
second greatest soccer game ever made, apart from
playing Goal on the Amiga 500 (side to side not
up and down). But nobody does that anymore so
Pro Evo will have to do...*
Konami, 2005

Midnight Club 3: Dub Edition
*'Club Foot' appears on this car racing game from
the makers of the notorious* Grand Theft Auto
series.
Rockstar Games, 2005

WRC: Rally Evolved
'Club Foot' used in intro to this car racing game.
Sony Computer Entertainment, 2005

Sing Star Rocks!
*'Club Foot' is on the tracklisting of this PS2
karaoke-based game*
Sony Computer Entertainment, 2006

Mark Echo's Getting Up Contents
Under Pressure
*Club Foot (Instrumental) / Club Foot (Mega
Mix)*
*You're a graffiti artist having all sorts of crazy
adventures ...*
Atari 2006

Tony Hawks Project 8
*'Club Foot' is on the soundtrack for the eighth
instalment of the hugely successful skate game.*
**Neversoft / Shaba Games / Page 44
Studios, 2006 / 2007**

SELECTED
COMPILATIONS

NME Presents Rock N Roll Riot 1:
Kicking Off
*'Cutt Off (NME Version)' on this cover-
mounted CD, the first of rather more compilation
appearances... take a deep breath...*
CD Covermount – NME, 2003

Evening Standard: London Fashion
Week, London Rocks
'Club Foot (Live At Cabinet War Rooms)'

included on this free CD given away with the
Evening Standard newspaper on September 23,
2004. It also features an 'enhanced' section
which includes 'Running Battle' and 'I.D.' in
Winamp format.
CD Covermount – Evening Standard, 2004

Q Magazine Best Of 2004

'L.S.F.' (Lost Souls Forever') is on this free CD
given away as a covermount with Q Issue 221,
December 2004.
CD Covermount – Q Magazine, 2004

Oorgasm 19

'L.S.F. (Lost Souls Forever)' included on this
covermount CD on the front of Dutch electronica
magazine, Oor in December 2004.
CD Covermount – Oor Magazine, 2004

Lara Croft Tomb Raider: The Cradle
Of Life

Features 'Reason Is Treason'
CD – Hollywood Records, 2004

The Cornerstone Player 055

Massive 3CD promo designed round the release
of 'Team America: World Police' and featuring
'L.S.F. (Lost Souls Forever)'
CD – Cornerstone Player 2004

Trax Sampler 079

Kasabian's ubiquitous 'L.S.F. (Lost Souls
Forever)' sneaks onto this French sampler of
electro and techno artists. Crossover? Not 'arf.
CD – Trax Records 2004

Festival

'Cutt Off' this time, from Warners' 2005
compilation of the greatest festival bands of the
period. And you can't have one of them without
the Leicester boys now can ya?
Double CD – Warner Strategic Marketing
UK, 2005

Goal! Music From The Motion Picture

The audio release of the soundtrack. Features
'Club Foot'. Which is quite apt, really.
CD – Big Brother, 2005

Holiday Hangover '05

What's up Smythe-Gillington? Darnit Jemima!
We missed a pre-festival compilation! Tell ya
what, let's buy a post-festival one. Oo, great
idea! Let's hope Kasabian's on there! Quality!
How about 'Reason Is Treason, Live From
Brixton Academy'? Let's get it! Great! More

champagne? Nah, I'm up early to play on
MySpace all day. Are you sure man? That'll
never catch on! Yeah, I know, I'm reading a
book about it that I bought for 30p on eBay and
I already want my money back.
CD – RCA, 2005

Revolutions: Radical Bands Alternative
Music

Kasabian are in good company here, with other
acts here including The Clash, Manic Street
Preachers, The Killers and loads more. Tracks are
'Club Foot' and 'Processed Beats' from the
Brixton Academy gig.
Double CD – Sony BMG Music
Entertainment (UK) Ltd, 2005

The Smart Club

Nova International, Elefant, Timid Tigers,
Kasabian ('L.S.F. (Lost Souls Forever)) – it can
only be a spiffy German compilation release can't
it?
CD – Panatomic, 2005

Twisted

Now this is a good 'un: 'Processed Beats'
features alongside such names as The Killers,
Mylo, Deep Dish, Scissor Sisters, Spektrum, The
Rapture and, uh, Bodyrockers on a compilation
of alternative mixes, remixes and damn good
shit.
Double CD – Vertigo, 2005

Music From The O.C.: Mix 5

'Reason Is Treason' is featured on this
compilation of tracks used in that U.S. T.V.
series. Doesn't that period look weird next to
that colon, by the way?
CD – Warner Brothers/WEA, 2005

Le Talent S'Ecoute En Son Et En
Images

Using an online translator for this and you get
'The Talent Is listened In Its And Images',
which is ace innit? A French compilation which
gathers in everything from 'Empire' (audio, and
video) to Evanescence, Ben Kweller and Sandi
Thom, who wants to be a punk rocker with
flowers in her hair, which is nice for her.
CD / DVD – Sony BMG Music
Entertainment (France), 2006

Now That's What I Call Music 65

You know you've made it when you're on one of
these. 'Empire' is, so they have.
Double CD – Virgin Records, 2006

Une Rentree, 2006

'Shoot The Runner' included here on this French release which also takes in the Long Blondes, Scissor Sisters, Chamillionaire and a host of French acts on a covermount for issue 563 of the magazine.

CD Covermount – Les Inrockuptibles, 2006

BBC Radio One Established 1967

Kasabian contribute a cover of The Specials' 'Too Much Too Young' to this compilation which celebrated forty years of the iconic radio station by getting contemporary acts to cover influential songs of that period. Sometimes, they're even good, too.

Double CD – Universal Music TV, 2007

Eddy Temple-Morris: Dance Rocks

'Club Foot: Eddy Losers Remix' appears on this cracking compilation from long-term collaborator / schemer / bro. Check out the label name…

CD – Botchit & Scarper, 2007

Radio One's Live Lounge – Volume Two

'Empire' included on this collection of acoustic and cover versions from the Live Lounge with which the boys became so familiar…

Double CD – Sony BMG Music Entertainment (UK), 2007

Mark Ronson: Version

A collection of reworkings of various famous tracks, featuring a splendid reimagining of 'L.S.F. (Lost Souls Forever)'.

CD – Red Ink, 2007

SELECTED SOUNDTRACK / TV APPEARANCES

Lara Croft Tomb Raider: The Cradle Of Life

Features hidden LP track, 'Reason Is Treason (Jacknife Lee Mix)' on this, one of the greatest films of all time. If you watch it with the sound off. And fast forward through all the bits without Angelina Jolie in them.

Paramount Pictures / Mutual Film Company, 2003

Goal!

AKA Goal! The Dream Begins (US)
Danny Cannon's re-telling of the basic rags-to-riches poor-boy-done-good Roy Of The Rovers

type tale features 'Club Foot' on its soundtrack amidst a slew of cameo appearances by contemporary footy gods. It's not as good as Escape To Victory, *but it is pretty smart.*

Touchstone Pictures, 2005

Green Street

'Club Foot' used in trailers for this film, and 'Stuntman' in the movie proper about footy hooligans that asked viewers to see Elijah Wood as a major 'face' on the scene.

Baker Street/Odd Lot Entertainment, 2005

Serenity

'Club Foot' used in trailers for this Joss Wheldon sci-fi romp. Hur hur. Romp.

Universal Pictures, 2005.

The Guardian

'Club Foot' crops up again on this Kevin Costner / Aston Kutchner vehicle.

Beacon Pictures, 2006

John From Cincinatti

'Sun/Rise/Light/Flies' is played over the credits of episode 101 of this TV series.

HBO, 2006

ITV 2006 World Cup

Kasabian's cover of David Bowie's 'Heroes' was used in highlights packages

ITV, 2006

Top Gear Series 9

'Empire' used by Clarkson and the boys

BBC2 – and repeats everywhere all the time. I love my satellite TV and it loves me back.

Match Of The Day

MOTD love tracks from that first album don't they?

BBC – all the darn time.

PARADISE RECORDS CATALOGUE NUMBERS

The Factory-esque propensity of numbering every release version / demo / promo on their own designated sub-label is a feature of the band's career and ownership of the various versions hereof was and is a badge of honour for Movement Originals and überfans alike. Here's a list of 'em all, and some of the extra goodies that came with them…

01 Processed Beats Demo CD
02 Processed Beats 10"Vinyl *Includes Kasabian flag*
03 Reason Is Treason Promo CD (Jacknife Lee Remix) *In brown paper bag*
04 Reason Is Treason 10"Vinyl *Includes Kasabian stencil*
05 Club Foot Promo CD *Includes B&W foldout poster*
06 Club Foot (Jagz Kooner Vocal Mix) 12" Vinyl *Two versions exist: the original white sleeve & white label of the first batch sent out to DJs as promo, and the second send-out in a navy blue sleeve.*
07 Club Foot (Temple Of Hell Remix) 12" Vinyl
08 Club Foot CD Single
09 Club Foot 10"Vinyl *Includes large double-sided poster*
10 L.S.F. (Lost Souls Forever) Promo CD *Hand-stapled blue paper sleeve with perforated sticker sheet*
11 L.S.F. (Lost Souls Forever) 12"Vinyl
12 Kasabian: Album Promo (CD-R) *Some are copy-protected*
13 L.S.F. (Lost Souls Forever) CD Mini
14 L.S.F. (Lost Souls Forever) CD Maxi
15 L.S.F. (Lost Souls Forever) 10"Vinyl
16 Kasabian: Album CD *A promo version of this – sans catalogue number - exists omitting the 'interlude' tracks, and featuring a red Kasabian figure, rather than a white one. The album proper notoriously featured DRM...*
17 Kasabian: Album DVD+
18 Kasabian: Album 10"Vinyl (Two LPs)
19 Processed Beats Promo CD/CD-R
20 Processed Beats CD Mini
21 Processed Beats CD Maxi
22 Processed Beats 10"Vinyl
23 Processed Beats (Afrika Bambaataa Remix) 12"Vinyl - White Label
24 Cutt Off Promo CD
25 Cutt Off CD Mini
26 Cutt Off CD Maxi
27 Cutt Off 10"Vinyl
28 Club Foot Promo CD (Re-release)
29 Club Foot CD Mini includes a live B-Side: 55
30 Club Foot CD Maxi
31 Club Foot 10"Vinyl
32 Live at Brixton Academy DVD *Unreleased*
33 Live at Brixton Academy - Download
34 Empire Single Promo CD
35 Empire (Album) Promo CD

36 Empire (2 Track CD Single)
37 Empire (Album) CD
38 Empire (Album) 10"
39 Empire (Album) CD Special Edition
40 Empire Single 10" *Includes Jagz Kooner Remix*
41 Empire Single DVD
42 Shoot The Runner CD Promo
43 Shoot The Runner CD Single
44 Me Plus One CD Promo
45 Shoot The Runner 10"
46 Shoot The Runner DVD
47 Me Plus One CD Single
48 Me Plus One Enhanced CD Single
49 Me Plus One 10"
50 Unknown
51 Fast Fuse 10" Promo

BOOTLEGS

Largely because Kasabian have an admirable and extremely modern propensity for offering oodles of free downloads of a huge amount of live and session goodies as well as interviews from around the world, the concept of The Bootleg is rather blurred in context here. However, there are a vast number of live and recorded demos and gigs available unofficially on the internet should you choose to search for additional and often lower-quality material (see websites section). Please remember that Home Taping Is Killing Music, File Sharers Have Small Willies (Or Will Grow One If They Are Ladies To Start With), S/He Who Smelt It Dealt It etc etc

Saracuse
Studio Sessions List
I'm not aware of the following rarities being available *anywhere* so here's a list of some of the more interesting things for which to hunt.

December 1998:
What's Going On / Interlude / Life Of Luxury / Shine On

Session 2: 1999:
Highest Number / Ten Past Three / In & Out Satellite / Dirty Dishes / Angels (Acoustic) / Come Back Down (Bedrock Studio Mix)

Session 3: 1999:
Full band tracks: *Pump It Up / Excuse To Get Wasted / Get Around / Stupid, Nothing Matters / You Won't Forget Me* Plus acoustic

demos of: *Come Back Down / Just Relax / Keep It Safe / Sniffing Glue / The Federation / The Warrior*

Session 4: September 21, 2000:
Rain / Come Back Down / Some Fingz In My Jeans / Somewhere Nowhere / Sun Ain't Gonna Shine / Wait For You Now / What Love Plus acoustic demos of: *Same Old Story / Lost Soul*

All four of the above sessions were recorded at Bedrock Studios, Leicester, and all remain unreleased to date.

Kasabian Selected Demos

Kasabian Bink Bonk Session, 2001
Processed Beats / Rain On My Soul / Beneficial Herbs
Recorded at Bink Bonk Studios, Bristol

Kasabien (sic) Demo, 2001: *Processed Beats / Rain On My Soul / Gone So Far (Bedrock Studio Mix)*
Note: 'Processed Beats' recorded at Bink Bonk Studios, Bristol with the other two tracks from various sessions in Bedrock. Some pressings to journalists featured an early version of the 'Kasabian man' with the name mis-spelt on the on-body text as 'Kasabien'. Arguably, Saracuse went into the studio, and Kasabian came out…
CD-R - 2000

Processed Beats
Note: This is the much-sought Demo CD featuring a 'case' of two pieces of cardboard held together by elastic bands)
CD / 10" - PARADISE 01 / 02

Reason Is Treason 10"
Note: The Jacknife Lee Remix that set the clubs astorm…
CD / One Sided 10" Vinyl: PARADISE 03 / 04

Downloadable bootleg compilations

Kasabian: The Acoustic Collection:
Processed Beats / L.S.F. (Lost Souls Forever) / Butcher Blues / 55 / Test Transmission / The Doberman (Serge Vocals) / Shoot The Runner / I'm So Tired (Beatles Cover) / Me Plus One / British Legion / Empire / The Doberman (Tom Vocals)

Note: Downloadable unofficial compilation of selected acoustic versions of Kasabian tracks

Kasabian RMXD: *Club Foot (Jagz Kooner Vocal Mix) / Reason Is Treason (fakeID mix) / Processed Beats (Afrika Bambaataa Mix) / Cutt Off (Mad Action Remix) / L.S.F. (Lost Souls Forever) (Jagz Kooner Mix) / Ovary Stripe (Band Remix) / Club Foot (Temple Of Hell 12" Remix) / Empire (Jagz Kooner Remix) / Shoot The Runner (Shakes Remix) / Me Plus One (Jacques Lu Cont Mix) / Empire (Alex C Remix)*
Note: Downloadable unofficial compilation of selected remixes

Kasabian Vs. The World: *Bus Stop Runner (Go Home Productions Remix) / By My Side (One Look Hooked Mix) Club Foot (Eddy Temple Morris Losers Remix) / Club Foot (Mr Grim Remix) / Empire (Alex C Remix) / L.S.F. (2006 White Label Mix) / L.S.F. (Ali dBass Remix) / L.S.F. (DJ Blair Electro Mix) /L.S.F. (Drum & Bass Remix) /L.S.F. (Pulse Remix) / L.S.F. (Teals Remix) / L.S.F. (Lost Souls Forever) [Creme Prulee Remix] / Mark Ronson Ft Kasabian : L.S.F. (Lost Souls Forever) / Processed Beats (Freaks Instrumental) / Processed Beats (Freaks Remix) /Reason Is Treason (fakeID Mix) /Reason Is Treason (Kriminalz Remix) / Shoot The Empire (CJ Horton Remix) / Kasabian v Beastie Boys - Club Shot / Kasabian v Blur - There's No L.S.F. / Kasabian v Ce Ce Penniston - Finally Stuntman /Kasabian v Daft Punk - Processed Funk / Kasabian v De La Soul - Processed Ring /Kasabian v DJ Kool - Processed Throat /Kasabian v Gravediggaz - Nowhere To Hide / Kasabian v Gravity Sounds - Music Is Mine (Demo) / Kasabian v Johnny Cash - Hurt The Doberman / Kasabain v Kelis - Get I.D. (McSleazy Remix) / Kasabian v Khyzer Zuke - Big Groovy L.S.F. / Kasabian v LCD Soundsystem - Everybody Is Listening In / Kasabian v M.I.A. - L.S.F. (Lionel's Galang Vinyl Remix) / Kasabian v Mylo - Herbs Four Hundred / Kasabian v Mylo v Beastie Boys - Drop The Club Life / Kasabian v Paradox 3000 - Processed Breaks / Kasabian v Primal Scream - Loaded Souls Forever / Kasabian v Sporadic-e - L.S.F. (the Pokerface Remix) / Kasabian v The Chemical Brothers - Chemical Feet / Kasabian v The Chemical Brothers - Galvanised Foot / Kasabian v The Music v Stone Roses - Breakin' My Bloody Process / Kasabian v The Prodigy - Poisoned Lost Souls*

/ *Kasabian v The Stone Roses - Processed Waterfall /Kasabian v The Timelords - The Doctor's Empire / Kasabian v Vitalic - My Friend Treason (IDC Remix) /Kasabian v Whitney Houston - Emotional Treason (team9 Mix)*

Note: For what it's worth, you can find these tracks collated in one place as a downloadable bootleg if you look hard enough. Essentially, a collection of remixes and mash-ups of the boys' stuff. Some official, some semi–official and some absolutely awful *My First Cubase* trainwreck territory, 'written' (in the loosest sense of the word) by a host of club DJs, home enthusiasts and a clearly a few weirdos. This ain't even a definitive list, neither. There's a point to be made here about the inherent flexibility of creativity or some such shit, but actually when it comes down to it the percentage of truly talented artists doesn't change, as this compilation illustrates.

SELECTED DIGITAL BOOTLEGS / GIGS / SESSIONS

The following is **a *selected list of live recordings, radio sessions, video footage and TV appearances*** that might be available for the dedicated fan

to track down on the internet, plus tracklistings *where available.* These tracklistings do not necessarily correspond to the full running order of the event, gig, or TV appearance – rather, they are indication of which tracks & excerpts are available, many of which were originally downloadable from the radio station / relevant websites for a limited period. Similarly, the titles here are the original ones as noted by the particular original audio or video provider. I mean, if there was one. Like, if someone *watched it live after paying to get in and then told everyone about what they'd seen.* Which last time I checked is legal. Anyway it goes without saying that nobody condones this kind of thing, so if you do accidentally end up finding and downloading any of these, stick a postal order for a couple of quid in an envelope and send it to the band. Or buy them a drink when you see them. Or a vintage Lineker-era match programme. Enjoy!

2004

AOL Session Reading Backstage 27.08.04: *Processed Beats / L.S.F. (Lost Souls Forever) / Butcher Blues*

Atomic Cafe Munich 29.10.04: *I.D. / Cutt Off / Processed Beats*

BBC Radio 1 Live Lounge Session 11.10.04: *Processed Beats (Acoustic) / Out Of Space*

Jo Whiley in charge here… she looks a bit like an ex-girlfriend of mine, you know.

BBC Radio 1 One Big Weekend 19.09.04: *Processed Beats / Reason Is Treason / Running Battle / Cutt Off / 55 / L.S.F. (Lost Souls Forever) / The Nightworker / Club Foot*

BBC Radio 1 One World 03.06.04: *Omnichord / Reason Is Treason (Fake ID Mix) / U-Boat / L.S.F. (Lost Souls Forever) / I.D. / Processed Beats*

BBC Radio 1 Zane Lowe Session 06.04.04: *Processed Beats / Reason Is Treason / Club Foot*

BBC Radio 6 Gideon Coe Session 29.07.04

Bowery Ballroom NYC 18.11.04: *Club Foot / L.S.F. (Lost Souls Forever) / Ovary Stripe / Processed Beats*

Brixton Academy 15.12.04: *Pinch Roller / I.D. / Processed Beats / L.S.F. (Lost Souls Forever) / Club Foot*

Frank Skinner Show 16.12.04: *Cutt Off*

Hull University 25.11.04: *Cutt Off / Reason Is Treason / Running Battle / Processed Beats / 55 / Test Transmission / L.S.F. (Lost Souls Forever)*

Oui FM Acoustic Boogie Nights 08.12.04: *Processed Beats / L.S.F. / Test Transmission*

Preston Mill 11.05.04: *I.D. / Processed Beats / Reason Is Treason / Running Battle / L.S.F. (Lost Souls Forever) / Test Transmission / Club Foot*

Reading Festival 27.08.04: *55 / Club Foot / Cutt Off / I.D. / L.S.F. (Lost Souls Forever) / Ovary Stripe / Processed Beats / Reason Is Treason / Running Battle*

Shibuya-Ax, Tokyo 01.11.04: *I.D. / Cutt Off / Reason Is Treason / Running Battle / Processed Beats / 55 / Test Transmission / Butcher Blues / Nightworkers / L.S.F. (Lost Souls Forever) / U-Boat / Ovary Stripe / Club Foot*

Summer Sundae 14.08.04: *I.D. / Processed Beats / Reason Is Treason / Ovary Stripe / 55 / L.S.F. Lost Souls Forever / Club Foot*

T In The Park 10.07.04

V Festival 22.08.04: *Processed Beats / Interview / L.S.F. (Lost Souls Forever)*

XFM Islington Academy London 10.11.04: *Reason Is Treason / Processed Beats / L.S.F. (Lost Souls Forever) / Butcher Blues / Club Foot*

XFM Session 29.07.04: *L.S.F. (Lost Souls Forever) / Processed Beats / I.D.*

XFM Winter Wonderland 5.12.04: *Reason Is Treason / Cutt Off / Processed Beats / 55 / L.S.F. (Lost Souls Forever) / Club Foot*

2005

ACL Festival Austin Texas 23.09.05: *Intro / Reason Is Treason / Cutt Off / Test Transmission / 55 / Butcher Blues / The Nightworkers / Processed Beats / Stuntman / L.S.F. (Lost Souls Forever) / Ovary Stripe / Club Foot*

BBC Radio 1 Maida Vale 13.01.05: *I.D. / Cutt Off / Reason Is Treason / Running Battle / Processed Beats / 55 / Test Transmission / Nightworkers / L.S.F. (Lost Souls Forever)*

BBC Radio 1 One Big Weekend 10.06.05: *Reason Is Treason / 55 / Test Transmission / L.S.F. (Lost Souls Forever) / Club Foot*

Benicassim Festival 07.08.05: *I.D. / Cutt Off / Reason Is Treason / Test Transmission / 55 / Nightworkers / Processed Beats / Stuntman / L.S.F. (Lost Souls Forever) / Club Foot*

Canal + Paris 28.01.05: *Processed Beats / L.S.F. (Lost Souls Forever) / Club Foot / Reason Is Treason / Cutt Off / Nightworkers / Running Battle*

Session broadcast February 5, 2005 except the latter two tracks

Cleveland Grog Shop 20.07.05: *The Stuntman / 55*

Festival Sudoeste Portugal 05.08.05

Friday Night With Jonathan Ross 25.03.05: *Club Foot*

Glastonbury Festival 26.06.05: *Pinch Roller / I.D. / Cutt Off / Orange / Butcher Blues / Processed Beats / L.S.F. (Lost Souls Forever) / Ovary Stripe / U-Boat / Club Foot*

Henry Fonda Music Box LA 12.03.05

KEXP Acoustic Session 09.09.05: *Interview / 55*

Kool Haus Toronto 20.05.05: *Pinch Roller / I.D. / Cutt Off / Reason Is Treason / Test Transmission / 55 / Butcher Blues / Processed Beats / Nightworkers / Stuntman / U-Boat / Ovary Stripe*

L'Agora d'Evry, Evry, France 10.01.05: *Cutt Off / Reason Is Treason / Running Battle / Processed Beats / Nightworkers / L.S.F. (Lost Souls Forever) / Club Foot*

Last Call With Carson Daly, NBC 20.09.05: *Reason Is Treason*

Lee's Palace Toronto 26.02.05

Leeds Festival 27.08.05: *Reason Is Treason / Cutt Off / Test Transmission / Processed Beats / L.S.F. (Lost Souls Forever) / Club Foot*

Lollapalooza Festival 24.07.05: *Pinch Roller / I.D. / Cutt Off / Reason is Treason / Test Transmission / 55 / Butcher Blues / Nightworkers / Processed Beats / Stuntman / L.S.F. (Lost Souls Forever) / Ovary Stripe / Club Foot*

Montreux Jazz Festival 06.07.05: *Pinch Roller / I.D. / Cutt Off / Reason Is Treason / Test Transmission / 55 / Butcher Blues / Processed Beats / Nightworkers / Stuntman / U-Boat / Ovary Stripe*

o2 Wireless Festival 30.06.05: *Reason Is Treason / L.S.F. (Lost Souls Forever) / Club Foot*

Oxygen Live Tent Acoustic Session 09.07.05: *Processed Beats / L.S.F. (Lost Souls Forever)*

Radio Eins Live Koln Prime Club 21.01.05: *I.D. / Cutt Off / Reason Is Treason / Running Battle / Processed Beats / 55 / Test Transmission / Butcher Blues / Nightworkers / L.S.F. (Lost Souls Forever) / Ovary Stripe / Club Foot*

St Andrews Hall, Detroit 27.02.05: *I.D. / Cutt Off / Reason Is Treason / 55 / Processed Beats / Nightworkers / Ovary Stripe / L.S.F. (Lost Souls Forever / Club Foot*

The Clubhouse, Tempe Arizona 12.06.05: *Introduction / I.D. / Cutt Off / Reason Is Treason / Test Transmission / 55 / Butcher Blues / Processed Beats / Nightworkers / Stuntman / L.S.F. (Lost Souls Forever) / Ovary Stripe / Club Foot*

T In The Park 10.07.05: *Stuntman / L.S.F. (Lost Souls Forever) / Cutt Off*

The Edge Session (103.9) 15.03.05

The End Session (107.7) 07.03.05

2006

1 Leicester Square (UK TV Show) 09.09.06: *Empire / Interview / Shoot The Runner*

4Music presents...Kasabian 28.08.06: *Intro / Empire / Interview (Part 1) / By My Side / Shoot The Runner / Interview (Part 2) / Processed Beats*

Interviews by Edith Bowman in this 4Music special on the band.

AOL Session Rock In Rio 03.06.06

AOL Session 11.09.06: *By My Side / Empire / Last Trip (In Flight) / Me Plus One / Stuntman / Shoot The Runner / Interview*

BBC Electric Proms 28.10.06: *Introduction / Shoot The Runner [Ft Zak Starkey] / Reason Is Treason / Empire / Me Plus One / By My Side / Processed Beats / The Doberman / Club Foot / L.S.F. (Lost Souls Forever) [Ft Zak Starkey]*

BBC Radio 1 Live Lounge Session 08.11.06: *Interview Part 1 / Shoot The Runner (Bluegrass Cowboy Version) / Interview Part 2 / Interview Part 3 / Somebody To Love (Jefferson Airplane Cover) /Interview Part 4*

Jo Whiley in the hotseat for this one.

BBC Radio 1 Maida Vale 26.07.06: *Empire / Reason Is Treason / Sun/Rise/Light/Flies / Shoot The Runner / Cutt Off / By My Side / Last Trip (In Flight) / Processed Beats / The Doberman / Club Foot / Stuntman / L.S.F. (Lost Souls Forever)*

BBC Radio 2 Session 04.11.06: *Interview 1 / Interview 2 / The Doberman (Acoustic) / Interview 3*

The boys chat to Jonathan Ross.

BBC Radio 2 Session 26.08.06: *Intro / Club Foot / Empire / Interview / Pictures Of Matchstick Men (Status Quo Cover) / Shoot The Runner*

Dermot O'Leary, who looks like my mate Woody, presented this one.

BBC Radio 6 Hub Session 22.08.06: *Empire / Shoot The Runner*

C4 Transmission Session 04.08.06: *Empire / Interview / Shoot The Runner*

Canal + 07.11.06: *Empire / Interview*

Europe 2 France Acoustic Session 05.11.06: *Shoot The Runner / British Legion / Processed Beats*

Ibiza Rocks Bar M, Ibiza 12.08.06

Jonathan Ross Show 20.10.06: *Shoot The Runner*

Kerrang! Radio Winners Session 08.06: *L.S.F. (Lost Souls Forever) / Shoot The Runner*

La Maroquinerie Paris 08.09.06: *Intro /Shoot The Runner / Reason Is Treason / Sun/Rise/Light/Flies / Cutt Off / Empire / Me Plus One / By My Side / Butcher Blues / Last Trip (In Flight) / Processed Beats / The Doberman / Club Foot / Stuntman / L.S.F. (Lost Souls Forever)*

Later...With Jools Holland 10.11.06: *Empire / Shoot The Runner / Club Foot*

Manchester Evening News Arena 11.12.06: *Intro (Clockwork Orange) / Brown Acid (Part 1) / Shoot The Runner / Reason Is Treason / Sun/Rise/Light/Flies / Cutt Off / Me Plus One / By My Side / Empire / Seek & Destroy / British Legion / Processed Beats / Last Trip (In Flight) / The Doberman / Apnoea / Club Foot / Stuntman / L.S.F. (Lost Souls Forever)*

MTV Studios, Camden Town 08.06: *Club Foot / Stuntman / Shoot The Runner / Reason Is Treason / L.S.F. (Lost Souls Forever) / Empire / Processed Beats*

First broadcast 21.08.06 on MTV

Neumo's, Seattle Washington 16.10.06: *Intro / Shoot The Runner / Reason Is Treason / Sun/Rise/Light/Flies / Cutt Off / Empire / Me Plus One / By My Side / Last Trip (In Flight) / Processed Beats / The Doberman / Club Foot / Stuntman / L.S.F. (Lost Souls Forever)*

Nottingham Arena 15.12.06: *Clockwork Orange (Intro) / Stay Away From The Brown Acid (Part 1) /Shoot The Runner / Reason Is Treason / Sun/Rise/Light/Flies / Cutt Off / Me Plus One / By My Side / Empire / Seek & Destroy / British Legion / Processed Beats / Last Trip (In Flight) / The Doberman / Encore / Apnoea / Club Foot / Stuntman / L.S.F. (Lost Souls Forever)*

Rock In Rio Festival Lisboa, Bella Vista Park 03.06.06: *Reason Is Treason / Sun/Rise/Light/Flies / Cutt Off / Me Plus One / Test Transmission / By My Side / Last Trip (In Flight) / Processed Beats / The Doberman / Club Foot / Stuntman / L.S.F. (Lost Souls Forever)*

T In The Park 08.07.06: *Reason Is Treason / Sun/Rise/Light/Flies / Processed Beats / Club Foot*

The Album Chart Show 21.10.06

The Koko (NME Birthday Gig) 12.09.06: *Clockwork Orange (Intro) / Shoot The Runner / Reason Is Treason / Sun/Rise/Light/Flies / Cutt Off / Empire / Me Plus One / By My Side / Butcher Blues / Last Trip (In Flight) / Processed Beats / British Legion / The Doberman (Ft Noel Gallagher) / Club Foot (Ft Noel Gallagher) / Stunman / L.S.F. (Lost Souls Forever)*

V Festival Chelmsford 19.08.06: *Shoot The Runner / Reason Is Treason / Sun/Rise/Light/Flies / Cutt Off / Empire / Last Trip (In Flight) / Processed Beats / Club Foot / Stuntman / L.S.F. (Lost Souls Forever)*

XFM Live At Leicester 04.09.06: *Shoot The Runner / Reason Is Treason / Empire / The Doberman / L.S.F. (Lost Souls Forever)*

Note: The tracklist above refers to official iTunes release which was UK only, included here as it has therefore subsequently inevitably widely bootlegged for and by overseas fans. Here's the full set: *Shoot The Runner / Reason Is Treason / Sun/Rise/Light/Flies / Cutt Off / Empire / Me Plus One / By My Side / Butcher Blues / The Last Trip / Processed Beats / The Doberman / Club Foot / Stuntman / L.S.F. (Lost Souls Forever) / Outro With Clint Boon*

XFM Radio Session 03.11.06: *Empire / Last Trip (In Flight) / Interview*

That Richard Bacon eh? Used to be on Blue Peter ya know.

XFM Winter Wonderland 12.09.06: *Shoot The Runner / Sun/Rise/Light/Flies / Me Plus One / Empire / The Last Trip / The Doberman / Club Foot / Stuntman / L.S.F (Lost Souls Forever)*

Y-Rock On XPN Session 22.09.06: *Interview Part 1 / The Doberman (Acoustic) / Interview Part 2 / British Legion (Acoustic) / Interview Part 3*

2007

AB Box, Brussels Belgium 14.02.07: *Me Plus One*

BBC Radio 1 Big Weekend 19.05.07: *Reason Is Treason / Shoot The Runner / Me Plus One / Empire / Processed Beats / The Doberman / Club Foot / Stuntman / L.S.F. (Lost Souls Forever)*

BBC Radio 1 Live Lounge Session 18.05.07: *Intro / Interview Part 1 / Empire*

(Acoustic) / Interview Part 2 / Interview Part 3 / Me Plus One (Acoustic) / Outro

Jo Whiley session.

BBC Radio 2 Maida Vale 09.03.07: *Introduction / Shoot The Runner / Sun/Rise/Light/Flies / Me Plus One / Empire / Last Trip (In Flight) / The Doberman / Club Foot / Stuntman / L.S.F. / Outro*

Janice Long session.

C4 Transmission Session 20.04.07: *Me Plus One (Acoustic) / British Legion*

Glastonbury Festival 22.06.07 (TV Broadcast)

Glastonbury Festival 22.06.07 (HD Broadcast)

Glastonbury Festival 22.06.07 (Webstream Broadcast): *Interview / Intro / Shoot The Runner / Reason Is Treason / Cutt Off / Me Plus One / Empire / I.D. / Last Trip (In Flight) / Processed Beats /The Doberman / Club Foot / L.S.F. (Lost Souls Forever) / Outro*

Green Energy Festival Dublin Castle 05.05.07: *Intro / Shoot The Runner / Reason Is Treason / Sun/Rise/Light/Flies / Me Plus One / Empire / Processed Beats / Apnoea / Club Foot / Stuntman / L.S.F. (Lost Souls Forever) / Outro*

Hammersmith Palais 13.02.07: *Shoot The Runner / Reason Is Treason / Sun/Rise/Light/Flies / Cutt Off / By My Side / Me Plus One / Empire / Seek & Destroy / Processed Beats / Last Trip (In Flight) / The Doberman / Apnoea / Club Foot / Stuntman / L.S.F. (Lost Souls Forever)*

Isle of Wight Festival 09.06.07: *Shoot The Runner / Cutt Off / L.S.F. (Lost Souls Forever)*

iTunes Festival 31.07.07: *Intro / Shoot The Runner / Reason Is Treason / Sun/Rise/Light/Flies / Me Plus One / Empire / Processed Beats / Last Trip (In Flight) / The Doberman / Club Foot / Stuntman / L.S.F. (Lost Souls Forever) / Outro*

Note: Full version of the gig at London's ICA that was subsequently made available for official download release through iTunes.

La Musicale with Emma De Caunes (Canal +) 19.01.07: *Empire / Shoot The Runner*

Lille Zenith 24.02.07: *Shoot The Runner / Reason Is Treason / Sun/Rise/Light/Flies / Cutt Off / By My Side / Me Plus One /*

Empire / Seek & Destroy / Processed Beats /
Last Trip (In Flight) / The Doberman / Apnoea
/ Club Foot / Stuntman / L.S.F. (Lost Souls
Forever) / Outro

Live '07 (NME Awards, Album Chart
Show)

Live Earth, Wembley Stadium 07.07.07:
Empire / Club Foot / L.S.F. (Lost Souls
Forever / Backstage Interview

Lowlands Festival (Full Gig) 17.08.07: Intro
/ Shoot The Runner / Reason Is Treason /
Cutt Off / Me Plus One / Empire / I.D. /
Processed Beats / The Doberman / Club Foot /
Stuntman / L.S.F. (Lost Souls Forever)

Lowlands Festival Acoustic Session
17.08.07: Empire / Processed Beats / The
Doberman

More 4 Presents... Live At Abbey Road
19.01.07: Interview 1 / Empire / Shoot The
Runner / Interview 2 / Me Plus One

Recorded October 25, 2006

MTV Japan Presents… Club Empire
11.01.07: L.S.F. (Lost Souls Forever) /
Interview

Planeta Terra Festival, Sao Paulo 11.11.07:
Reason Is Treason / Cutt Off / Empire / I.D.
/ Processed Beats / Fast Fuse / L.S.F. (Lost
Souls Forever)

Showcase Acoustic Session Paris 23.02.07:
Me Plus One / Processed Beats / British
Legion / L.S.F. (Lost Souls Forever)

Somerset House 13.07.07: Intro With Danny
Dyer / Empire / Interview Part 1 / Shoot The
Runner / Interview Part 2 / Club Foot /
Interview Part 3 / L.S.F. (Lost Souls Forever) /
L.S.F. / Outro / Comments

Summersonic Festival, Tokyo 12.08.07:
Shoot The Runner / Club Foot / Empire /
Stuntman

T In The Park 08.07.07: Shoot The Runner /
Sun/Rise/Light/Flies / Me Plus One /
Empire / Processed Beats / Stuntman / L.S.F.
(Lost Souls Forever) / The Doberman / Club
Foot

Note: Running order may be incorrect

Taratata France 4 Session 20.01.07: Shoot
The Runner / Someone To Love (Jefferson
Airplane Cover) / L.S.F. (Lost Souls Forever)

Teenage Cancer Trust, The Royal Albert
Hall 29.03.07: I.D. / Processed Beats / Last
Trip (In Flight) / Club Foot / Stuntman /
L.S.F. (Lost Souls Forever)

Tennent's Vital Festival, Belfast 22.08.07:
Shoot The Runner / Reason Is Treason / Cutt
Off / Me Plus One (Intro) / Me Plus One /
Empire / I.D. / Processed Beats / The
Doberman / Club Foot / Stuntman / L.S.F.
(Lost Souls Forever)

J's The Athena Cinema Leicester 26.07.07:
Shoot The Runner / Empire / Club Foot / Me
Plus One / L.S.F. (Lost Souls Forever)

V Festival, Chelmsford (as broadcast on
Channel 4 festival coverage, UK, 2007):
Interview / Empire

Yokohama Blitz Arena 13.01.07: Stay Away
From The Brown Acid (Part 1) / Shoot The
Runner / Reason Is Treason /
Sun/Rise/Light/Flies / Cutt Off / By My
Side / Me Plus One / Empire / Seek &
Destroy / Processed Beats / Last Trip (In
Flight) / The Doberman / Apnoea / Club Foot
/ Stuntman / L.S.F. (Lost Souls Forever)

BOOKS AND AUDIO BOOKS

The ABC Book
Audio Books - Ladybird Books
Humpty Dumpty
Audio Books - Ladybird Books
Both Recorded and Mixed at Bedrock Studios, Leicester during March / April 1998

According to Scott Gilbert of Bedrock Studios, "Chris [Edwards] sourced the FX for me, and we both played mice; his mum & sister did most of the script." The first official release of any of the Kasabians... squeak squeak.

Guest Appearances and Oddities

Engeltarre – Come On You Engletarre
Unofficial England song for Euro 2000, on which members of Kasabian apparently can be found shouting in the chorus.
MP3/CD Promo – No label, 2000

Wash And Go – Will You Go To Bed With Me?
Unreleased 1999 recording - Tom Meighan and Chris Edwards, folklore has it, guest as solo kazooists on this obscure but great version of the equally obscure-but-equally-great track.

DJ Shadow – The Outsider
Serge Pizzorno and Chris Karloff appear on the album track, 'The Tiger'
CD/LP – Island Records, 2006

Processed Strings: The String Quartet Tribute To Kasabian: *Club Foot / Processed Beats / I.D. / Test Transmission / Butcher Blues / Cutt Off / L.S.F. (Lost Souls Forever) / Ovary Stripe / Reason Is Treason / Running Battle / U-Boat / Bad Hand*
Note: As the title suggests, an album of string interpretations of Kasabian tracks, plus one original song, 'Bad Hand', courtesy of Tallywood Strings
CD – Vitamin Records (USA), 2006

WEBSITES

A search on your search engine of choice shall indeed turn up some good stuff. And, whilst we're at it, searching on your social networking site of choice will unearth the unofficial pages of the band, individual members, fan groups and the like. No point listing them all here, I think we're all familiar with MySpace, Facebook etc by now. If you're not familiar with MySpace, Facebook etc you should buy Whose Space Is It Anyway?, *a fine book which is available from www.impbooks.com and features a lot of marvellous pictures and some swearing, too. Where were we? Oh yeah. Websites. Here's a small selection. There are lots more, I'm sure.*

www.kasabian.co.uk
Official website with very lively message boards and a host of downloads for those quick enough off the mark.

http://club-empire.blogspot.com/
Excellent resource for audio, television appearances, rarities and the like. Every single person who visits this site goes on to buy every single official piece of merchandise, apparently.

http://messiahfortheanimals.blogspot.com/
See above…

http://www.kasabianweb.com/
Unofficial fansite
http://kasabianempire.proboards104.com/index.cgi
AKA The Empire Of Kasabian – linked directly from Kasabianweb, this is another message board with a committed set of posters.

www.kasabiandownload.com
Nicely designed.

http://www.h6.dion.ne.jp/~ultrapop/kasabian/index2.html
Marumi's excellent Japanese fansite, which is called Cutt Off

http://kasabian-france.easyforum.fr/login.forum?connexion
French site.

http://www.kasabianblog.splinder.com/
And one for our Italian cousins – absolutely loads of live gigs, TV appearances and so on to play with.

http://kasabianitalia.it/
Massi's excellent Italian website fizzes with energy and information.

Visit our website at *www.impbooks.com* for more information
on our full list of titles including books on:

Robert Plant, Slash, Damon Albarn, Bernard Sumner,
MC5, Dave Grohl, Muse, The Streets,
Green Day, Ian Hunter, Mick Ronson,
David Bowie, The Killers, My Chemical Romance,
System of a Down, The Prodigy and many more.